HOW TO MAKE YOUR OWN BUILT-IN FURNITURE

HOW TO
MAKE YOUR
OWN BUILT-IN
FURNITURE
BY PERCY BLANDFORD

TAB BOOKS
Blue Ridge Summit, Pa. 17214

FIRST EDITION

FIRST PRINTING— DECEMBER 1976

Copyright © 1976 by TAB BOOKS

Printed in the United States
of America

Hardbound Edition: International Standard Book No. 0-8306-6910-8

Paperbound Edition: International Standard Book No. 0-8306-5910-2

Library of Congress Card Number: 76-45057

Preface

Built-in furniture is a product of the age. It suits the modern way of life. Besides its attractions in terms of space saving, capacity, and utility, built-in furniture can be used to express individuality. In contrast, quantity-produced free-standing furniture, which may be attractive both in price and quality, is the same as other people have. Most of us have to accept this, as the cost of craftsman-made furniture puts it beyond reach except for the few with the necessary skill to make their own free-standing furniture.

Although there are pieces of built-in furniture that can be bought as quantity produced units, there are limits to what can be done along these lines. Building in inherently means that the shape and size of the available space has to be taken into account and the furniture made accordingly. It is here that the home owner and amateur craftsman gets an opportunity to exercise his skill in producing an individual item of furniture. Fortunately, built-in furniture is generally simpler to make than free-standing furniture, as the face is about all that is visible; the surrounding walls form a large part of the construction.

As nearly all built-in furniture has to be designed to suit a particular situation, stock designs can only have limited value.

Consequently this book is more than a series of designs. What is of more use to anyone looking for information on built-in furniture is information on tool handling, detailed construction work, and basic design considerations, and some suggestions of things to make that can be adapted to suit circumstances. That is what this book is all about, and I hope a great many readers will find enough information between these covers to move them to tackle more ambitious furniture projects than they previously thought they were capable of.

Percy W. Blandford

Contents

The Planning Stage

Not so very long ago the amount of built-in furniture in many homes was small—possibly a few shelves in an alcove, or a small ready-made rack or storage unit hung on screws. In a modern home, built-in furniture is much more extensive, and in some rooms there may be more fixed furniture than free-standing items (ones that can be moved about).

TO BUILD IN, OR NOT TO BUILD IN

Of course, there are advantages and disadvantages of built-in furniture, but for most purposes the advantages outweigh the disadvantages. There are many considerations—not all immediately obvious—and this chapter is concerned with weighing the pros and cons, then generally planning how built-in furniture is to be arranged. The rest of the book tells how to make it.

Advantages of Built-In Furniture

The term *built in* can be applied to any furniture item that is fixed in place. Sometimes its attachment is only incidental, and the item is otherwise little different from a piece of free-standing furniture. This points to one reason for building in. If there is a risk of furniture being knocked over or moved from position, there is a good case for fixing it to the wall or floor, or both. A tall glass-fronted display cabinet could be vulnerable if unattached, and the result of knocking it over could be breaking the crockery on display. That risk is completely removed by building in.

Besides giving rigidity and security to a piece of furniture, building it into a corner, an alcove, or merely against a straight wall usually simplifies its construction. The wall—and often the floor and ceiling—becomes part of the structure. Only nominal framing may be needed on the contact surfaces; wall, ceiling, etc.) or if a more solid surface is needed, this can be simpler and cheaper to build than if the furniture is to be visible all around.

Choice woods are often difficult to get and very costly, but built-in furniture lends itself to the use of manufactured boards. It is possible to use ordinary particle board or chipboard for internal parts, plywood or hardboard for parts against a wall or otherwise hidden. For faces these materials can be bought already veneered or covered with Formica or similar plastic. These prepared boards can be very attractive, yet their use in some free-standing furniture would seem inappropriate.

Another good reason for built-in furniture is economy of space. In an alcove something built in will be the maximum size that can be accommodated, so its capacity will be as great as possible. A piece of free-standing furniture, even if specially made to go into place, will be smaller by a few inches all around.

Free-standing furniture, even if fairly close fitting in a recess or corner, will collect dust around the neighboring surfaces, so periodically the furniture will have to be withdrawn for cleaning. Its built-in counterpart will have none of these dust traps. Close-fitting free-standing furniture will have its meeting surfaces hidden for most of the time. This means that parts made of choice wood will not be seen, so part of the article might be considered wasted. Of course, the table, cabinet, bookcase, or other thing can be removed at some later time and used elsewhere—something that cannot be done with built-in furniture. However, there is the possibility that the shaped parts will be a different color than those that have been exposed to light.

In general. most built-in furniture is easier to make than most free-standing furniture. Some of the outline is already there as fixed surfaces of walls. floor. and ceiling. Parts can be prefabricated to fit or can be made and fitted in position. Usually parts of the structure are made up as units and fitted in place. then the next part is made. Though poor craftsmanship is always to be deplored. one may make an internal part of a piece of built-in furniture to much less than perfection and it will not matter. Of course. the exposed surfaces must be as well made as in any other piece of furniture. but the need for highest quality workmanship throughout is much less in built-in furniture.

Storage Space and Built-In Furniture

Most pieces of furniture are made to serve a need. They may also provide decoration. but their prime purpose is utilitarian. Things like chairs and tables are normally better for being movable. although a fixed tabletop sometimes may be more convenient than a free-standing table. (There are examples of built-in desks. folddown tables. and similar things elsewhere in this book.) Seating can sometimes be built in—possibly around a window alcove—and the lower part can become storage space.

It is just this feature—storage space—that is often better provided by building in. Bookshelves are obvious examples. A greater capacity for books can be provided by simple shelves fixed to the wall than by any type of free bookcase. In a kitchen. worktops on built-in furniture that match the appliances can be much more convenient than a collection of free-standing items. They also make better use of the space in what is often not a very large room.

Even against a straight wall. fixed furniture takes up less floor space than comparable free-standing items. If the built-in article is arranged as a complex serving many purposes— storing books. providing a cocktail cabinet. housing a desk with stationery storage. and providing display space—it will take the place of several other pieces of furniture and thus free other floor and wall space. This may be even more of an advantage in a bedroom, where free floor space is sometimes minimal once the bed has been positioned. A combined unit with clothes closet, dressing table, and other services can be attractive and can take care of the occupant's needs in a way that would be difficult or impossible otherwise.

If there are recesses or alcoves, building into them may be the only way of making good use of them. Otherwise they may become depositories for odds and ends in an untidy jumble. They may still store these things, but shelves, a top, and a door will bring order out of chaos and make these areas look much better.

Building in also has some effect on insulation and problems of heating or cooling. Built-in furniture gives extra thickness to the wall it adjoins, and this provides an extra barrier to heat or cold—particularly important along an outside wall. In some situations insulation material may be included in the back of the furniture to increase this effect.

Building in is more final than making free-standing furniture. A built-in piece becomes part of the house, unless you make it in a take down form. If you own the house and intend to live there for a long time, this may be a good thing. If you expect to move in the near future, it is necessary to weigh up the value of the furniture to you for the period you will be there and estimate how much it will add to the value of the house when you sell. If the house is not yours, you have to allow for the fact that you will have to leave the built-in furniture behind—without getting anything for it—if you move.

Even if the furniture is not a permanent fixture and you can dismantle it and take it with you, it will have been designed for a particular situation, and it may not be much use, without considerable alteration, in another home. This is particularly so with corner or alcove items in which corners are sometimes far from right angles. Furniture which goes against a flat wall is more adaptable.

PLANNING FOR BUILT-IN FURNITURE

You have to be satisfied that a particular piece of built-in furniture is what it is wanted, and in the right place and the right size, before you make and fit it. In most cases alterations are not easy, and producing something that proves to be unsuitable often means scrapping it and starting over. Early sketches are worthwhile, and it may be better to make a rough mockup of what is intended from card and scrap wood so that others concerned can see what is intended and agree to its construction. This may also show flaws in design. It could be that the proposed item would interfere with natural lighting, prevent a room door from opening, or do something else undesired. Such problems should be taken care of before work is started on the actual piece of furniture.

High Storage

A place where built-in furniture scores high over free-standing furniture is high in a room. Free-standing furniture is usually not very tall. A clothes closet may be high enough for the clothes to hang above one or two drawers and the top may still be far enough from the average ceiling to leave a space which could be useful, yet storage there results in an untidy pile. With built-in furniture the whole room height can be used.

A Basic Plan

Of course, ceiling-height storage may be too high for anyone standing on the floor to reach, but this is an opportunity to use space that is otherwise wasted, and it can house things that are only infrequently wanted. There can be bookshelves to suit reference books and others that are only needed occasionally (Fig. 1-1A). There could be cupboards with doors that hinge normally, slide, or swing up (Fig. 1-1B).

One of the attractions of making built-in furniture is that it is possible to make combined pieces that have several functions. An example is in a bedroom (Fig. 1-1C). In this case, just about everything is taken care of around the bed, but a room has four sides, and it is not good design to put everything to one side. In this case, the window is to the left side, and a free-standing dressing table is the main feature of the wall facing the foot of the bed. A stool for the dressing table and a chair make up the furnishings.

Fig. 1-1. Wall space out of arm's reach can be converted to occasional storage space for things seldom used, by building in bookshelves (A) or cupboards (B); one of these could be constructed above the doorway of the bedroom shown (C).

This sort of thing does not design itself; there has to be some preliminary work, probably with several experimental layouts, before a pleasing result is achieved. If you are artistic you may simply sketch views as you hope they will appear, but you may find that, although your sketch looks good, the pieces won't fit in the available space. More design information is given later in the book as it relates to various items of furniture, but broadly the approach should be as follows.

A plan of the room is drawn to any suitable scale. The walls concerned are drawn, and any doors or windows marked. In the example, the walls at the head of the bed and by the door are involved (Fig. 1-2A). The bed and other things that will stand on the floor are also drawn to the same scale on card and cut out. You will have to decide how wide you would like the bedside cabinets and how large the clothes closet will have to be for what you want to put in it. Sizes may have to be modified later, but move the pieces around on the floor plan to settle positions (Fig. 1-2B). Consider the movement of doors. Will the clothes closet door clear the bed (Fig. 1-2C)? If not, the bed will have to be moved, and this affects the bedside cabinets, making one wider and the other narrower. If there just is no way for the closet door to swing, you will have to settle for sliding doors.

Also consider the room door. If it happens to be hinged on the side against the clothes closet, will it swing far enough? If not, the clothes closet may have to be moved, affecting the bedside cabinet, or it will have to be made narrower.

Fig. 1-2. The plan for a bedroom should include a drawing of the proposed placement of furniture against walls (A), cardboard furniture models that can be moved around on a floor plan for experimental positioning (B), and allowance for closet door swing (C).

Having arranged the things on the floor to apparent satisfaction, how will they look against the walls? At the wall at the bed head, draw the bed, add the two cabinets, and allow space for the inset shelf that the clothes closet will determine. There could be a problem with the bedside cabinet that comes next to the clothes closet. If drawers are used, they must have the near edge far enough out to clear the front of the clothes closet, and even then they can only be used when the closet door is closed. Will this suit your needs? If at some time you think there is a risk of someone pulling out a drawer against a partly open closet door and doing damage, would it be better to have a door on the cabinet, or merely shelves that could never lead to collision with the closet door?

At the other wall the closet can be drawn in and a block of shelves arranged over the end of the bedside cabinet. If there is a worthwhile space between the top of the door and the ceiling. it might be better to carry the upper part over the door (Fig. 1-3A). If this is not worthwhile. the better plan might be to stop at the closet side (Fig. 1-3B).

Fig. 1-3. If possible, high cupboards should be carried as far as possible across a wall for the best use of space, even over a doorway (A); otherwise, cupboard construction will have to stop at the door (B).

The high storage space at the head of the bed probably looks best if it is at a matching height with the top compartments of the closet. as illustrated in the upper right hand portion of Fig. 1-1C. It does not have to be, but if the bottom edge is brought lower. what about the door near the corner fouling the closet door when that is opened? If both are hinged in the same corner. there is not much risk; but if the upper door swings the other way or upwards. it could strike the opened closet door. Sliding doors would avoid this. but sliding doors do not give as clear as access to the interior.

There is yet another problem. which is common to all built-in furniture that goes around a corner. What do you do where the two parts meet? At the top. one cupboard could be carried through (Fig. 1-4A). or there could be a mitered division (Fig. 1-4B). If the lower part is not to be wasted space, there has to be access. If the bedside cabinet has a door or shelves. it could be carried through. If there are drawers, any access that way might only be possible by withdrawing the drawers. giving what almost amounts to a secret compartment. but that is not what is usually wanted. There could be a lifting top over the corner. making this suitable for storage blankets and similar things. or it might be used for soiled linen (Fig. 1-4C). Another way would be to cut off the clothes closet wall so access is from inside the closet. The space might then be used for shoe storage (Fig. 1-4D).

Fig. 1-4. Rows of cupboards that meet at a corner can overlap (A) or they can be separated by a mitered partition (B). No amount of space within built-in furniture should be left over; you can usually find a way to get to the extra space in a dresser (C) or closet (D).

This seems to take care of most aspects of planning the layout in this case. After your first drawings of the floor and two walls have been experimented on, there may be many lines that are not wanted and might confuse you when construction work starts. At this stage it is advisable to trace over what is wanted and discard the original so there can be no risk of using the wrong drawing.

One final step in the planning stage is to arrange a simple mockup in the actual room. Position the bed where you intend it to be. If the floor is bare, mark where the other things are to come with chalk. If this cannot be done, lay down strips of wood to indicate outlines. Pivot other pieces of wood on nails to represent doors, and see that they have ample clearance. Use some scrap pieces of card, hardboard, or plywood as drawers and try pulling them in and out to see that nothing will come in their way.

Reasons for Planning

All of this may seem a lot of planning, but it is really just a logical reasoning through of the requirements involved and how they will be met. In most built-in furniture, except the simplest, the alteration of one part has to be matched by the alteration of another. It is obviously better to check all this and arrive at a satisfactory result before wood is cut and joints are made. Once construction goes ahead it is frustrating to find

19

that something has been overlooked and you have to alter some wood and scrap other parts.

It can also be frustrating when making something like this bedroom furniture. in which many parts make up the whole, to find thatsomewhere along the line a measurement is wrong. It might only be a slight error where two parts that should be level are about ⅛ in. off, possibly not much more than the thickness of a pencil point against a rule. It could be a larger error perhaps. due to forgetting to allow for the *plinth*, or the thickness of a strip under a top, when measuring. This is human error and may happen to any of us, but the risk is reduced by using a *rod*. A rod is a strip of wood with key dimensions marked on it. In the example, it would be a strip of wood reaching from floor to ceiling. Prominently marked on it

Fig. 1-5. It's always best to use a rod (wooden gauge) for marking out the placement of furniture parts. Errors are often made in reading rules.

are such things as the height of the plinth. the level of the cabinet tops. and the lower edge of the high units (Fig. 1-5). Measurements with rods and other devices are discussed more fully in the next chapter.

Measuring And Marking

The best method of measuring is to compare one part with another. If the piece to be marked to size can be placed against a part it is to match and marked from it. there is no need to bother about feet and inches. Direct comparison reduces the risk of error to a minimum. This does not mean various measuring rules and tapes do not have a place—they are very important—but their purpose is to provide a means of comparison. and the woodworker, whether making new parts or repairing old ones. should look for ways of cutting out intermediate measuring steps.

MEASURING

As we are in a world transition of measuring systems, any craftsman should be prepared to measure in feet and inches or in metric measure. This means rules and tapes that are bought should have markings in both systems. It is extremely unlikely that metric measure will completely replace the traditional measure for several generations. Even if there is a determined attempt to use metric measurements for new work, there will have to be reference to things that were made or built to the older system; and where they come in a round number of inches or feet. any conversion may result in unwieldly figures.

For instance, the familiar 2 by 4 in. section is 51 by 102 mm. While new stock may be machined to 50 by 100 mm, combining the sizes in a structure could result in growing errors, or at least a slack fit. On things of larger size—such as an 8 by 4 ft. plywood sheet, which converts to 2438 by 1219 mm—some modification of stock size will come to give a round figure, but much existing design suits the older measurment. All of this means that woodworking craftsmen will have to be aware of possible differences and and be prepared to adjust their measured work accordingly.

Linear Measurements

A folding rule is convenient for carrying. Most are quite thick, so if they are put flat on a surface, the graduations are high above the surface. This could result in errors of parallax (sighting). To avoid this, the rule should be put on its edges to bring the markings close to the surface (Fig. 2-1A). While a pencil dot may be all that is needed, it is a help in locating the marks later if they are *pecked* as shown in Fig. 2-1B, the point of the V being the measurement point.

Fig. 2-1. Putting a rule (A) on edge (B) avoids errors of parallax.

Much of the work of the folding rule has been taken over by the tape rule, which stows compactly in its case and usually has a hooked end. This is likely to be the most frequently used measuring instrument in furniture work.

The folding and tape rules cannot be used for drawing straight lines and are not the most convenient tools for setting gauges or tool fences. Straight steel rules are better for these uses. Although a 12 in. rule is usual, a 24 in. or 60 mm one is better for bench work, both for accurate measuring and for drawing straight lines. Turned on edge it can also be sprung to curves that have to be drawn.

Most woodworkers use ordinary round pencils for marking wood. The point quickly blunts and frequent sharpening is necessary. The life of the point can be lengthened if it is sharpened to a chisel shape. Rub the point on a piece of fine glass paper glued to a strip of wood to maintain this shape.

The traditional carpenter's pencil has a rectangular-section lead in oval-section wood. This sharpens to a broad chisel point that has a long life. These pencils are worth buying if they can be found.

For greater accuracy, particularly where a cut is to be made across the grain, a knife may be used instead of a pencil. The usual knife has been one with an angled cutting edge across the end. A newer type has disposable blades and has other uses besides marking.

Dividers (Fig. 2-2A) may be thought of as only a means of scratching circles, but they are also valuable for comparing measurements and for stepping off distances. If rungs or rails

Fig. 2-2. Dividers (A) are useful for stepping off distances (B) as well as drawing circles, while calipers (C and D) are needed for measuring curves.

have to be equally spaced, using dividers will ensure accuracy (Fig. 2-2B).

Calipers are really dividers with bent ends. The outside caliper (Fig. 2-2C) is used for checking across curves. A piece turned on a lathe cannot be measured across with a rule, but calipers can be adjusted to it and checked against a rule or the part the lathe-turned part is to fit. Inside calipers (Fig. 2-2D) serve the same purpose in hollows or holes.

Angular Measurements

The checking and measuring of angles—particularly right angles—occurs frequently in woodworking. The basic tool for marking and testing right angles is a *try square* (Fig. 2-3A). This may be all steel or may have a brass-faced wooden stock and a steel blade. The check for accuracy is to press it against a straight edge. draw a line along the blade, and then turn it over and see that the blade still matches (Fig. 2-3B). Try

Fig. 2-3. The accurate marking and checking of angles is done using the try square (A and B), combination square (C), and bevel (D).

squares are made in many sizes. For general work it is worthwhile having one with a 12 in. blade. Instead of a smaller try square it may be better to have a *combination* square. The

24

head can be locked anywhere on the blade so the blade length can be adjusted to suit what is needed. The other side will mark or test a miter of 45° (Fig. 2-3C).

For angles other than 45° or 90°, an adjustable *bevel* is needed. This has a blade which slides in its stock and can be locked at any angle and extension (Fig. 2-3D). The bevel can be set to a protractor or an existing cut piece.

MARKING

Lines parallel to an edge can be drawn by measuring two or more points and then laying a straight edge through them, but in most cases it is better to gauge the line. To do this, a notched piece of wood is pulled along with a pencil against its end (Fig. 2-4A). An experienced woodworker can make a reasonably accurate line with the pencil between first finger and thumb and the other fingers against the side of the wood, but this is not recommended.

A combination square can be used in this way. With the blade set to the correct distance and a pencil held against the end, the square can be drawn along the edge (Fig. 2-4B). A marking gauge uses a similar idea with a scratching point. There are wood and metal marking gauges that can be used for distances up to about 6 in. from an edge. The gauge (Fig. 2-4C) is tilted towards the direction in which it is to be pushed.

Fig. 2-4. Gauges can be used to mark lines parallel to an edge.

25

The first finger curls over the top of the stock, the thumb pushes behind the point, and the other fingers keep the stock pushed against the edge of the wood.

A *mortise gauge* is similar but it has two points that can be adjusted in relation to each other as well as in relation to the stock (Fig. 2-4D). It scratches two lines at the same time and gets its name from its use in marking out mortise and tenon joints, but it has other uses. If used for a mortise, the chisel to be used is tried against the points so they are set to the correct width. The ordinary marking gauge scratches and may tear the grain. A cutting gauge has a knife blade, which makes a clean cut (Fig. 2-4E) and is particularly valuable for use across the grain. It will also cut parallel strips of veneer.

When almost all woodworking processes were done by hand, it was customary to prepare each piece of wood with a face side and face edge. These were the first side and edge, planed straight and at right angles to each other. They were identified by face marks (Fig. 2-5). Now that some processes are done more easily and more accurately by machine, there

Fig. 2-5. Matching surfaces should be marked (A) and mating joint parts numbered (B).

is not always quite such a need for face surfaces in all woodworking; but in furniture work a reasonable degree of precision is needed, and it is wise to use these marks. When a framework is being made, all marking is done from the face surfaces, with try square, marking gauge, and other tools used there, and not the other way. Then when the piece is assembled, all face marks are kept one way (usually outside). This results in correct matching on the face side, and any errors due to difference in thicknesses all come on the other side.

Coupled with this is the need to identify joints. Even when joints are cut mechanically, it is unlikely that all joints in a particular assembly could be interchangeable. This means that joints should be lettered or numbered. These marks are usually made so they come together then a part is unlikely to be reversed.

It is possible to have all surfaces apparently flat and all corners right angles but the work out of true. This is called *in winding*. An example is in a long board that is flat, as tested crosswise at several places, but twisted. The amount of twist can be more easily seen if a pair of winding strips are used. These are two matching strips of wood, thick enough to stand edgewise. One may have pieces of contrasting color insets at its ends to aid sighting. If these strips are placed at opposite ends of the board and sighted along, any twist can be seen (Fig. 2-6).

Fig. 2-6 Sighting across the edges of winding strips will show any twist in the board they're resting on.

Another twisting problem comes during assembly. Much furniture construction consists of frames built up and then joined to each to make a boxlike framework. If any part of this assembly is out of true, it becomes very apparent to any observer. Opposite sides should be made up first. When one is assembled, its corners should be checked with a try square, then by measuring diagonals (Fig. 2-7A). The second assembly is made face down on top of it to match. Both assemblies have to be checked for twist by sighting across them. Usually it is best to leave them under clamps or weights on a flat surface for the glue to set (Fig. 2-7B). If the box is longer one way, accuracy is usually more easily obtained if the long sides are assembled first.

When the other parts are fitted, check for squareness in the short sides and measure diagonals as well. It is then necessary to check for twist or winding across the assembly in both directions. If the assembly can be stood on a known flat surface, it can be held down under weights; but before this is done and before the glue sets, there must be a check of squareness when viewed from above (Fig. 2-7C), and probably

Fig. 2-7. Comparing the diagonal dimensions of a rectangular sub-assembly provides extra assurance of its geometric accuracy. Subassemblies being glued for a boxlike structure should be held under weights (B) to avoid warps; check a trail assembly for trueness (C) before final gluing.

from the bottom as well on many assemblies. Finally, stand back as far as you can and look at the assembly from several directions. You do not have to be very experienced to notice lack of squareness anywhere, and it is better for you to see it now and correct it than to leave it for a visitor to point out later.

Holding Devices

For most woodworking processes both hands are needed for things other than holding the wood, so the wood must be supported and held in a way that suits the operation. Although a limited amount of work can be done with improvised equipment, and there are sometimes occasions when it is necessary to make do with something that is not up to the desired standard, good craftsmanship is dependent to a very great extent on the way the wood being processed is held.

BENCH WORK

The first requirement is a bench. The important part is a stout, wide board for the front edge. This is usually of hardwood and is upwards of 2 in. thick to withstand hitting without noticeable bending. It may be supported by a front apron almost as thick (Fig. 3-1). The legs must be sturdy, and if the bench is free standing, it should be of sufficient size to resist turning over or moving. There is an advantage in building a bench onto a wall so that maximum rigidity is obtained.

If a bench is unavailable, a stout board may carry a vise and be clamped to a table, but this is much less satisfactory. A bench should be at a comfortable height for working, and for

← apron

Fig. 3-1. The heart of a woodworking shop is a rigid bench topped with thick hardwood that is supported by an apron.

the average person, this is about 30 in. There is an advantage in making it as long as the available space will permit. The greater the length, the easier it is to accommodate long pieces of wood and plane or otherwise work them accurately.

Besides the bench there is often a use for trestles, or sawhorses, preferably two of the same height. These are best at a height convenient for sawing, which means about 18 in. They need not be very well made, but they should be rigid. Old chairs without their backs are sometimes used, but it is better to make horses with the legs splayed wide to resist tipping (Fig. 3-2).

Fig. 3-2. Probably the most convenient height for a sawhorse is 18 inches. It need not be made neatly, but its legs should take a wide stance; a pair of sawhorses can support doors and other large pieces being planed.

For right-handed working, it is best to mount a vise towards the left end of the bench. A large professional-type vise with wood over the jaws is best (Fig. 3-3A). A quick-release action is what it says, but not essential. Smaller clamp-on vises may have their uses, particularly when work has to be done away from the shop, but good work is much easier with a substantial vise.

There should also be a bench stop. For planing and some other processes, the wood needs something to prevent it from sliding off the bench. Simplest is a strip of wood nailed across the bench end, but it is better to have something that can be adjusted out of the way. There are metal stops that recess into the top of the bench and can be adjusted up and down with a screw action. The objection to these is that they are metal; if a plane hits one. its blade is damaged. Many workers prefer a wooden stop because of this. A simple one is a tight fit in a hole through the bench and that can be forced up and down. An improvement is a screw and nut that lock the stop in position (Fig. 3-3B).

Fig. 3-3. The bench vise (A) and bench stop (B) are fixed devices used to hold and steady work.

Another essential piece of bench equipment is a bench hook. or preferably a matching pair (Fig. 3-4A). The hook is made to go over the bench as far as the edge of the front board, and the cross pieces are held with glued dowels rather than screws. so there is no metal for saw or other tools to touch.

The most common use of the bench hook is to press wood against it with one hand while sawing with the other. So that the saw does not drop through and damage the bench. one end can be cut back (Fig. 3-4B). If the wood being worked is long, the second hook provides additional support. It is probably advisable to regard the bench hook as consumable. Chopping with a chisel and other cutting can be done on it rather than damaging the bench top. The hook can be scrapped and replaced when it gets badly damaged.

When long pieces of wood are held in the vise. it is helpful to have holes to take pegs at the other end of the bench to provide support (Fig. 3-4C). If thin wood is to be planed on edge. this can be done more accurately if the wood is supported on the bench. A V-block (Fig. 3-4D) will steady the wood. If it has two dowels to fit holes in the bench top, it can be removed when it is not needed.

Fig. 3-4. One of the pair of bench books shown (A) has a recessed top piece (B) that allows a saw to strike its base rather than the bench. Dowels inserted into one of several holes in the bench (C) can give a vise a helping hand in holding work; the V-block (D) is another temporary wood-holding aid held by dowels.

Traditional hand-working cabinetmakers used a *shooting* (planing) *board* to hold wood to be planed on edge. Machine planing has superseded this method for production planing, but anyone making or repairing furniture should know about it. A long-soled plane is used on its side, and the wood is supported at about the height of the center of the blade. A shooting board may be 3 ft or more long and arranged with a block to hold in the vise (Fig. 3-5A). A smaller one could be made like a bench hook and used with a low-angle plane for squaring across the end grain.

If corners have to be taken off a square section, as when chamfering for decoration or preparing wood to turn in a lathe, a trough is valuable. Two pieces are beveled at about 45° and

Fig. 3-5. Planing aids.

fastened together, then a stop is recessed into them. A trough wider than it is deep (Fig. 3-5B) can rest on the bench top. It may have extension pieces for use when extra-long wood is to be worked on. If the rough is deeper than it is wide (Fig. 3-5C) it may be held in the vise.

CLAMPING

Clamps are needed in as wide a range as possible. The basic C-clamp (Fig. 3-6A) is used in many sizes for holding parts together while joining them or for holding wood while it is being worked on. A variation on the C-clamp has a sliding head (Fig. 3-6B). This increases the range, but usually the reach is not as great as in a C-clamp equal to its greatest capacity, so pressure cannot be applied as far from an edge. Wooden clamps with pairs of screws (Fig. 3-6C) have their uses, but they cannot exert as much pressure.

Fig. 3-6. A variation of the C-clamp (A) has a sliding head (B); a near kin to these is the wooden clamp (C).

A *bench holdfast* is a type of clamp likely to be frequently used. In its simplest form the stem goes through a hole in the bench top; then tightening the screw causes this to hold by leverage and friction. A better type has serrations in the stem to engage with matching projections in a metal collar recessed into the bench (Fig. 3-7A).

For clamping outside the range of C-clamps, there are *bar clamps* (Fig. 3-7B) sometimes called *sash* clamps from their original use in clamping sash windows during their making. Usually a pair of bar clamps are needed. Although a straightforward squeeze is all that is needed, a distorted assembly can be pulled true by setting a bar clamp slightly askew. There are heads similar to those on bar clamps available for fixing to the edge of a board, usually with pegs through holes, but these are not usually as effective as an all-metal bar clamp.

Fig. 3-7. The bench holdfast is aptly named: Its serrated stem grips a grooved collar imbedded in the bench. For work of a size beyond the capacity of a C-clamp, there is the bar clamp (B).

There are many improvisations that can be used for holding and clamping; most are based on a wedge action. A wedge pressing against a block can provide a considerable pressure (Fig. 3-8A). This is useful for holding laminations around a former. A similar action comes from a cam. A disk is given a lever and mounted on a screw through an off center hole (Fig. 3-8B). This acts as a rotating wedge.

A single wedge does not give a parallel action, so it may move parts being clamped. The remedy is to use a pair of "folding" wedges (Fig. 3-8C). If they are driven against each other, the pressure is tremendous and parallel This method can be used to make an effective bar clamp (Fig. 3-8D). The idea can be used on an assembly: A block of wood can be temporarily screwed to a part so a pair of wedges can work against it to provide pressure on another part (Fig. 3-9).

Fig. 3-8. Pieces being glued can be pressed together with a wedge action.

Rope and cord are used for clamping, sometimes with wedges. Rope knotted as tightly as possible around an assembly can have one or more wedges driven beneath it to exert more pressure. For a frame or other structure, the rope should be padded so as not to pull into the edges of the wood; shaped wood blocks are best (Fig. 3-10A).

Fig. 3-9. Wedges placed between one part of an assembly and a temporary stop nailed to another part.

Fig. 3-10. Rope can be tightened around parts being glued with wedges (A) or a Spanish windlass (B).

Another way of tightening a rope is to use a *Spanish windlass* (Fig. 3-10B). It can pull parts of a chair back together or put pressure on parts which have to be forced in to a curve. There is considerable strain on the cord, so it is usual to have many turns with the ends tied. A lever, often a hammer handle, is put in the turns and twisted. When pressure is sufficient the end of the lever can be lodged against a part of the structure or tied alongside the twisted cord.

Saws And Sawing

Sharp saws are essential to good work. The best sharpening or setting is done professionally by machine, although it is possible for the craftsman to maintain his own saws. In either case, it is obviously best to have saws that keep their edges as long as possible. This property is related mainly to the quality of the steel and the way it is tempered, and these things in turn are usually related to price, so it is always advisable to buy the best saws you can afford.

Much wood, particularly those varieties used for furniture, is bought already cut to section, and the craftsman making furniture is mostly concerned with saws that will cut wood to length and make joints. He is less concerned with the saws used to convert wood from the log or reduce the sizes of bulk lumber.

SAW TEETH

Two general forms of saw teeth are used—for those cutting across the grain and those for cutting along the grain. To provide clearance, nearly all saw teeth are set by being bent alternately each way so the *kerf* or cut, made in the wood is wider than the thickness of the steel plate from which the saw blade is made (Fig. 4-1A). Saws used on green wood (freshly felled and containing much sap) have considerable set, for a wide kerf; but even the fine saw used for small pieces of wood that are correctly seasoned must have some set unless the cut is merely superficial. Teeth for cutting across the grain must sever fibers with a knife action. Teeth for cutting along the grain cut with more of a chisel action. *Crosscutting* teeth can be used along the grain, although not as efficiently; they are commonly used for all directions when cutting joints.

Similar tooth shapes are used for handsaws and power saws, although power saws may be given gullets (channels) between groups of teeth to clear sawdust, and there are tooth shapes used on some power saws to give special characteristics. Many of these could not be applied to handsaws, as an electric motor has a reserve of power denied to the human muscles.

Saw teeth for cutting across the grain have an included angle of 60° (Fig. 4-1B), which allows for sharpening with a triangular file. The sharpening angle gives alternate teeth knifelike edges on opposite sides of the blade. Up to half the depth of each tooth is bent outward to give the width of the kerf (Fig. 4-1C).

Fig. 4-1. When a saw blade cuts, it makes a kerf wider than itself (A). The teeth for cutting across the grain (B and C) differ from those used with the grain (D).

The coarseness of saw teeth is defined as the number of points in an inch. The usual range of handsaws have teeth between 5 and 18 points per inch, although fine piercing saws may have many more, and large saws for cutting up trees may have fewer. Power saws tend to have coarser teeth than handsaws used for the same purpose.

Saw teeth for cutting along the grain also have an included angle of 60°; but the forward edge is nearer upright, and the teeth are filed straight across (Fig. 4-1D). Setting is similar to crosscut teeth, but often coarser because there is more of a tendency for the wood to bind on the sides of the saw.

HANDSAWS

The general-purpose handsaw for cutting on the bench is a *backsaw* (sometimes called a *tenon* saw) about 12 in. long and with 14 or 16 teeth per inch. The back is stiffened with a piece of steel or brass, and the handle may be wood or plastic. There are variations in handle forms, but the important thing is a comfortable one-hand grip with a thrust directed to somewhere near the middle of the cutting edge (Fig. 4-2).

Fig. 4-2. A properly designed backsaw applies thrust directed toward the middle of the cutting edge.

The best control is obtained with one finger held straight (Fig. 4-3). Most saws have their own slight perculiarities. A craftsman gets to know his own favorite saw and instinctively gives any necessary little bias to achieve an accurate cut.

For finer work there may be a smaller backsaw, sometimes called a *dovetail* saw, only 8 or 10 in. long, with 18 points per inch.

Panel Saw

Backsaws are mostly used for nearly horizontal cuts on wood held in the vise or on the bench hook. Usually the cuts are not of very great extent, although thin sheets of plywood may be conveniently cut for long distances with a backsaw. For cutting thicker wood or for other heavier and longer cuts, the proper tool is an ordinary *handsaw* or *panel* saw (Fig. 4-4).

Fig. 4-3. Using a backsaw to cut a piece of wood held against a bench hook. Note the first finger held alongside the handle to provide greater control.

Much of this sort of work can be done more easily with small powersaws, but a craftsman needs one panel saw for work the power saw cannot manage. A saw with a blade about 24 in. long and crosscut teeth, about eight per inch, should do.

Fig. 4-4. Using a handsaw. The wood is held by kneeling on it and steadying with the other hand. Note that the saw angle is slightly steeper than 45° and the first finger is held alongside the handle to give good control.

A saw of similar general appearance but with teeth for cutting along the grain is called a *ripsaw*. Whether one is needed or not depends on the type of work, but if hardwoods have to be cut by hand along the grain, this is much easier to use than a crosscut saw.

Although a panel saw may be used on the bench and can be made to cut down wood held in the vise, the usual method of use is to have the wood on one or a pair of horses and to kneel over the wood and saw downward at an angle. The angle of cut depends on the wood. If it is comparatively thin, it will cut more cleanly at a flatter angle, as more teeth will be in contact at one time; but if it is thick wood, the effort needed for each stroke is reduced if the saw is more upright, so that a shorter length of wood surface is presented to the saw at each stroke.

A point to watch in any sawing is that the method of support does not encourage the kerf to close on the saw as the cut progresses. It is better to saw wood supported at one side of the cut than between two supports. The free part should be held so it does not drop, and the last few strokes should be taken lightly so the grain fibers do not break out.

Handsaws for Curves

Ordinary saws can only make straight cuts or follow a very slightly curved line. Special handsaws for cutting curves have been largely replaced by power saws, but there are sometimes places where the power saw cannot reach or where the intricate shapes are better cut by hand.

Figure 4-5 contrasts the panel saw (A) with the curve-cutting handsaws. The type at B has a thicker blade to compensate for narrow width from teeth to back. These are sometimes called *compass* saws and may be supplied with one handle and a set of three or more blades of different widths for curves of different sizes. A very narrow saw of this type, which usually fits through a pad handle, is called a *keyhole* saw (Fig. 4-5C).

For anything finer than this, the blade has to be tensioned. A *scroll or coping* saw (Fig. 4-5D) has a sprung frame. The even finer *fretsaw* usually has a rather deeper frame. In both cases the blades are disposable, and several spares should be kept.

Fig. 4-5. A variety of saws are needed, ranging from a handsaw (upper left) to narrower saws needed for curves.

When using any saw on a curve, it is important to keep it cutting when altering its direction, or it may twist and break in the cut.

POWER SAWS

The power saw for straight cuts is a table saw with a circular blade. There are general-purpose blades, but if there is a great variety of work to be tackled, there will have to be several blades. One with crosscut teeth like those of a handsaw will make finer cuts and leave surfaces that need less finishing than a saw with larger combination teeth. A large saw is more generally useful than a small one. Of course, it should have ample power, as there is often a tendency to make such a saw do work really outside its capacity. Also, as teeth get blunt the load on the motor increases considerably. Either the saw spindle should have a rise-and-fall adjustment, or the table should have a similar adjustment.

For ordinary cutting, the maximum amount of blade should project. This puts less load on the motor than if the blade has less projection, because not so much saw edge is in contact with the wood at one time (Fig. 4-6A). There can be considerable overload if the wood is not fed straight, so the fence or other guide should be kept truly parallel with the saw. Much of the joint cutting that can be done by hand may also be done with a table saw by adjusting the depth of cut and fence distance (Fig. 4-6B). Angles may be cut with a suitable sliding guide (Fig. 4-6C) or adjustable fence (Fig. 4-6D) with a precision greater than that obtainable with a handsaw.

The alternative to pushing the wood against a rotating saw is to have the saw movable in relation to the wood. Such a saw may be completely portable, within the limits of its power cable (Fig. 4-7A), or it may be mounted to give a limited range of movements in a *radial arm* saw (Fig. 4-7B). While both saws have many uses, some of these are more applicable to carpentry than furniture making. A table saw is a better first choice.

Some modern furniture has fairly severe straight lines, but other modern furniture and most colonial and antique furniture includes plenty of curves. Anyone making

Fig. 4-6. The variations in height of a table saw (A and B) make it versatile. Adjustable fences permit the accurate cutting of angles (C and D).

reproduction pieces or repairing old furniture needs to be able to saw curves with reasonable accuracy if subsequent work with other tools is to be kept to a minimum. There are machine tools that make accurate sawing easier than with comparable hand tools.

Fig. 4-7. A portable power saw (A) is an alternative to a handsaw; a radial arm saw (B) differs from many other power saws in that it moves in relation to the wood.

Bandsaw

A *bandsaw* has a continuous flexible cutting band over two or three wheels. The depth of throat limits how far a cut can be made from an edge (Fig. 4-8), but even a small bandsaw can be made to cut curves in quite thick wood, providing progress is kept slow.

Fig. 4-8. A bandsaw uses a continuous blade running around wheels.

Blades are easily changed. A narrow blade is used to follow a tight curve. The strength of a wider blade can be used for bigger curves. A bandsaw can also be used for straight cuts. Although it does not have the ability to keep on its straight course without much guidance, it is convenient for short cuts.

Saber Saw

Another power tool for curves is the *saber saw*, which is moved in relation to the wood to be cut. The saber saw works with a reciprocating motion and cuts on the upward stroke. This means that any raggedness from the cut is on the top surface. (With a bandsaw it comes below.) The actual movement of the saw is not great, so although the blade might pass through wood 2 in. thick, it would not cut it very well, if at all. A saber saw is more suited to thinner wood. It does not have the bandsaw's limit of distance from an edge.

As saber saw blades are unsupported at one end, they have to be thick for stiffness. Different sizes and types ot teeth may be had. Coarse teeth are needed for thick and soft wood, but a better surface is obtained on hardwood with teeth as fine as can be made to cut the curve. There are saber saw blades to suit metals and plastics. The proper use of a saber saw is illustrated by Fig. 4-9.

Fig. 4-9. A saber saw uses a short blade with a reciprocating motion to saw curves.

Other Power Saws

An alternative saber saw is one in which the same type of blade points upwards through a table and the wood is moved against it. The cut is then downward, so the better surface from the cut is on top and it is easier to follow a line. Except that a saber saw is not restricted in the distance of the cut from an edge, a bandsaw is generally preferable, as cutting is more accurate and the cut edge is better.

There are power scroll saws or fretsaws, which will take the same blades as the hand frames. They are less popular than they once were, but anyone wishing to make the intricate pierced chair backs or other fretted work of some furniture styles will find these tools best for the purpose.

Tools And Techniques For Shaping And Smoothing

Anyone working on furniture needs a variety of chisels. These are end-cutting tools, and their effectiveness depends on their sharpness.

TYPES OF CHISELS

Common chisels come in widths from ¼ in., or less, upwards. The widest commonly needed is 1½ in. The general-purpose type often described as a *firmer* chisel, has a flat, parallel-sided blade.

Most new chisels have plastic handles that can be hit with a hammer or mallet, but traditional chisels had wooden handles and were hit with wooden mallets. Firmer chisels may be bought with a beveled edge (Fig. 5-1B) and these penetrate wood more easily and can get into corners. Longer and thinner versions are *paring* chisels, which are not intended to be hit.

A chisel curved in cross section is a *gouge*, and these come in similar widths. A gouge sharpened on the inside (Fig. 5-1C) is used for paring internal curves, and one sharpened outside (Fig. 5-1D) is used for hollowing. At one time, very stout mortise chisels were used for chopping out joints (Fig. 5-2), but it is more usual now to remove the bulk of the waste with a drill and do final shaping with firmer chisels.

Fig. 5-1. The chisel blade may be parallel edged (A), but it is more versatile if bevel edged (B). A gouge may be sharpened inside for paring (C) or outside for hollowing (D).

A large range of gouges in many widths and degrees of curvature are used for carving. There are a few carving chisels and tools of special form. but most tools in a carver's kit are gouges. A wood turner uses chisels and gouges, but

Fig. 5-2. Chisel and gouge ends. Left to right: a narrow firmer chisel, a wider bevel-edged chisel, a mortise chisel, a gouge ground outside with a rounded end for hollowing or turning, a gouge sharpened on the inside for paring.

these are longer and stronger than those used for other woodworking. and the handles are long to provide leverage. The gouge blade may be square across or rounded. It is thick and is sharpened on the outside (Fig. 5-3A). Turning chisels are sharpened on both sides and usually have skew ends (Fig. 5-3B).

Fig. 5-3. The roughing tool for turning wood on a lathe is a long gouge (A), the finishing tool is a chisel sharpened on both sides (B).

PLANES

Planes may be regarded as devices to control the cut of a chisel. A chisel may cut freehand to almost any thickness of shaving. but the plane restricts the cut to the removal of a comparatively thin shaving. Traditional wooden planes are just about obsolete. but if one becomes available, it is probably worth acquiring. The modern steel plane has lever and screw adjustments. as well as a sole which stays true (unlike a wooden plane. which had to be trued with another plane occasionally).

A plane may have a single *iron*, or blade (Fig. 5-4A), but most planes intended to produce a smooth surface also have a *cap iron* (Fig. 5-4B). (The word *iron* is still used despite the fact that parts are now being made of steel.) The cap iron breaks off the shaving into segments. and this discourages tearing up the surface of the wood.

Length of sole is an advantage when uneven wood has to be trued. A short *smoothing* plane might follow undulations, but a long plane bridges the hollows and takes off the high spots first (Fig. 5-4C).

A *jack* plane (the name comes from *jack-of-all-trades*) is the one for getting rough or sawn wood approximately to shape. The mouth of the plane is set fairly wide (there is usually a screw adjustment), and the blade is sharpened to a slight curve (Fig. 5-4D). The cap iron is set $\frac{1}{16}$ in. or more back from the cutting edge. The plane can be set to take off fairly thick shavings, but may not then leave a good surface.

Fig. 5-4. Simple planes have single irons, but most modern planes have a cap iron to break off shavings (A and B). To true an uneven surface, there is an advantage in a long plane (C). A plane's cutting edge may be rounded for rough and quick cuts (D) or straight with rounded corners for finishing (E).

· The long *trying* plane (one of several variations shown in Fig. 5-5) follows if there is need for truing in the length, and a smoothing plane removes roughness. In both cases the plane is set to only take off a fine shaving. The mouth is set narrow, and the cap iron is fairly close to the cutting edge, which is sharpened straight across, with the corners rounded.

A plane should be used, if you are right-handed, with the left hand on the knob and the right hand on the handle. The wood should be on the bench against the stop or in the vise so it is possible to stand against the side of the bench near the end of the wood and push the plane away from you. This gives the best control and achieves best results. Standing at the side of the work causes excessive strain on the muscles, and plane control is less precise.

A *block* plane is a one-handed tool about 7 in. long with a single iron set a a low angle. The better block planes have adjustable mouths. They are mostly used for cuts across the grain, but they are useful for any fine cut, such as taking the sharpness off an edge.

Fig. 5-5. A group of useful planes for hand work. Upper left: a long trying plane, a shorter jack plane, and a slightly smaller smoothing plane; all are similar in construction. A low-angle block plane for one-hand use across the grain is in front of the jack plane. In front: a plow plane for making grooves and a fillister for cutting rebates.

There are special planes for cutting rabbets and other grooves. An ordinary plane cannot go close into a recess, but if the iron runs the full width it can. There have been *rabbet* planes of ordinary appearance except for the cutting edge going full width, but most such planes are narrower. When given a fence to control depth and width of cut, the tool may be called a *fillister*. A plane for making a groove is called a *plow*. It has a narrow sole and a kit of blades of various widths, plus depth and side fences. Modern fillisters and plows are all metal, and there are combination planes that will do these and other jobs. However, power tools can perform similar functions and may be preferable.

At one time, any cabinetmaker had a large collection of *molding* planes, each with its bottom and blade shaped to the profile of a molding. Modern furniture has less molding, and what there is either bought ready-made and stuck on instead of being part of the base wood, or it is produced by a spindle molder or other mechanical means. Old molding planes would still have value in reproducing or restoring old furniture.

A simple plane for getting to the bottom of a groove, as in a dado joint, is little more than a chisel through a block of wood (Fig. 5-6A). This is an *old-woman's-tooth*, or router. A metal version has a bent blade with more of a cut than a scrape.

Most planes are used on flat surfaces only, although a plane with a flat sole can be used on an externally curved surface. There are planes known as *hollows* and *rounds* that are shaped to work straight edges of matching curved sections. Planes have been made with adjustable curved bottoms to work lengthwise hollows.

Fig. 5-6. A router (A) with a projecting blade levels the bottoms of grooves. A spokeshave (B) works curves.

For curves in the length there are *spokeshaves* (Fig. 5-6B). These have handles at the sides and a little cutter that may have adjustments like a plane. There may be a flat bottom for working external curved edges, or a rounded bottom for planing hollows. Much of the work of spokeshaves is now better done with a *Surform* tool, which may be flat or curved and is used like a file. Its cutter is a replaceable blade with a series of rasplike cutters which let the shaving pass through.

PLANING MACHINES

Planing machines have their uses in the home shop, but quite often their capacity is insufficient for all work undertaken. A planing machine has revolving cutters. The depth of cut is controlled by regulating the difference in height of the feed and takeoff tables. The size of the machine is the width of maximum cut. A planing machine can also be used at its edge for cutting rabbets. Some planing machines can be moved over the wood surface in the same way as a hand plane. Both types of machine certainly reduce labor. Manual planing hard and cross-grained wood can be very tiring.

Using the Planing Machine

Machine planing, by its nature, produces a series of curved indentations. If the wood is fed very slowly over the cutters, these will not be very obvious; but they would show through a finishing treatment if no other work were done on the surface. Although machine planing is often followed by sanding, it is better in good-quality work to remove all signs of machine planing by using a smoothing plane before sanding or other work. If the cutters of a planing machine are not in perfect condition, they may pound the surface as well as cut it, causing later unevenness or uneven absorption of stain or polish. Hand planing removes this risk.

Molders and Routers

Rotating cutters, power-driven at vry high speeds, have taken over from molding planes and other tools that worked recesses, rabbets, and patterns. As with most other power tools, there are static and portable versions. In the static version the motor is below a table, and the cutter projects above it in a space in an adjustable fence. Wood passed along the fence is cut with the reverse of the profile of the rotating cutter. This *spindle molder* can have plane cutters to make rabbets, or shaped ones to produce moldings.

The portable tool is called a *router*. The motor is on top and is fitted with handles. The cutter projects through a broad base, which is cut away to expose the cutter. There are depth adjustments, and various guides and stops can be used. The tool can be used to level the bottom of a groove or to make the groove without any need for sawing or chiseling first. A plain 1_2 in. cutter, for instance, can be led across a piece of wood, and the result will be a groove of even depth with clean sides. A guide can be used for straight or shaped cut, or the cutter can be guided around a marked line.

TOOL SHARPENING

Chisels and plane irons must have frequent sharpening if good work is to be done. Sharpening is done in two stages: (1) grinding, which is the removal of the bulk of the unwanted steel, and (2) honing, or whetting, which is the actual production of the cutting edge. Sharpening can be done many times with most tools before grinding becomes necessary again. With some tools, such as the thin irons in some planes, you may never need to resort to grinding. However, if there is much thickness of steel, grinding saves time and effort at the sharpening stage.

Some craftsmen have their tools ground professionally from time to time, but in most shops it is convenient to have a grinder. At one time this was a large sandstone wheel, turned slowly by foot or hand and kept moistened by dripping water. Modern grinding is usually done with a smaller, fast-turning grinding wheel which is used dry. The moistened sandstone wheel had the advantage of not drawing the temper of the steel.

When steel tools are made they are first hardened; then the degree of hardness is reduced enough to suit the purpose of the tool. If the tool is later heated so that colored oxides appear on the surface, further softening takes place. The amount of softening is indicated approximately by the area of colored oxidation. Although the oxides are easily rubbed off, the tool is only restored to condition by grinding past the area that was softened. When grinding on a high-speed dry stone, it is important to have a container of water nearby and dip the tool in this frequently.

Grinding

A chisel and the thicker plane irons are given two distinct bevels (Fig. 5-7A). The sharpening bevel starts quite narrow, then further sharpening widens it. After many sharpenings an unduly wide bevel is produced and the tool must be ground again. If the grinding is on a small wheel, the tool may be against the rest and the wheel circumference. It should be moved from side to side, particularly if the wheel is narrower than the tool edge. This minimizes overheating and grinds the edge evenly. If the tool is held continually at the same angle, the final bevel will be hollow (Fig. 5-7B). Slight hollowness may not matter, but it could result in weakness and either breaking or vibration in use; so it is better to move the tool up and down slightly during grinding to give a flatter bevel (Fig. 5-7C). If grinding may be done on the flat side of the grindstone, this ensures flatness (Fig. 5-7D), although there is more risk of grinding unevenly.

Fig. 5-7. On many woodworking tools there is a main grinding bevel and a shorter sharpening bevel (A). Grinding is done on a revolving stone (B through D).

Honing

Final sharpening is done on an oilstone. There are natural stones (such as Arkansas) and manufactured stones (such as carborundum). Usually the natural stones are finer than the manufactured ones, although it is possible to get double-sided manufactured stones with fine and coarse grits. A useful size for dealing with most tools is about 8 by 2 by 1 in. It is advisable to mount the stone in a wooden block. The oil used on the stone should be thin—sewing-machine oil rather than automotive oil.

Sharpening of chisels and plane irons for normal purposes is on one side only. There are guides which clamp to the tool and roll along, holding it at the correct angle. If the tool is sharpened freehand, one hand holds it and the other applies pressure (Fig. 5-8). The important thing is to maintain the same angle for the length of the stone. There is a tendency to

Fig. 5-8. Sharpening, or honing, a plane iron. The left hand controls the angle and direction, while the fingers of the right hand apply pressure as the plane iron is rubbed along the stone.

dip the hands at the far end of the stroke. Besides rubbing up and down the stone, it is advisable to move the tool about to keep wear on the surface even (refer to Fig. 5-9). Angles are only approximate.

The need for sharpening can be seen sometimes as a line of reflected light when the blunt edge is examined. Rubbing on the stone should be continued until this disappears. Wipe oil off the tool and examine the edge. When the side being sharpened has been rubbed down to nothing, a sliver of steel will be rubbed off. This is quite minute, but when seen across the

56

blade, it is a sure sign that sharpening has been achieved. It may be felt by sliding the finger gently down the flat side towards the edge. This *wire edge* is removed by rubbing flat on the stone a few time. To make sure it's gone, the edge is sliced across a piece of scrap wood.

hold

press

Fig. 5-9. Chisels and plane irons are sharpened on a flat stone.

For the best edge the tool is sharpened on a coarse stone completely, then the process is repeated on a fine stone. If the sharpened edge is examined under a microscope, it will reproduce the size of the grit in the stone in a sawlike edge. The coarser the grit, the faster it cuts; so sharpening on a coarse stone gets a reasonable edge quickly. But if a fine stone follows and is used enough to rub away all the marks of the coarse grit, the result is a better cutting edge.

Knives are sharpened in a similar way, except they are rubbed on the stone both sides. Carving gouges are often given a slight bevel inside. Turning chisels are sharpened on both sides, as a knife is.

The outsides of gouges can be sharpened on a flat oilstone by rolling the tool as it is rubbed. Insides have to be dealt with by an oilstone having a curved edge, or *slip*. There are several forms of these slips, usually with several sizes of curves on the same piece of stone. Usually the slip stone is rubbed inside the gouge like a file. An inside-sharpened gouge cannot be ground on a normal stone, so all of the sharpening inside is done with a slip, and the wire edge is rubbed off the outside with a flat stone. If it is the outside that is sharpened, the slip is only needed to remove the wire edge by rubbing lightly inside.

SCRAPING AND SANDING

Sometimes the grain is such that a smooth surface cannot be obtained by plane. The oldtime cabinetmaker scraped with a piece of broken glass, but a better tool is a steel cabinet scraper. This is a piece of saw steel. The edge is filed true, and both sides of this are turned over by rubbing very firmly either with a hard round steel rod or the flat of a chisel (Fig. 5-10A). The scraper is pushed to a slight curve and moved over the wood at an angle that makes the turned-over edge scrape a very thin shaving off the wood (Fig. 5-10B). There are handled

Fig. 5-10. By turning over the edge of a piece of steel (A), a scraper (B) can be formed.

scrapers that can be pulled over a surface for a similar effect; some have throwaway blades that ensure a good cutting edge without the sometimes awkward setting of the burr of the edge of a cabinet scraper. As wood with awkward grain is often used on furniture because of its attractiveness, scraping may be the only way of bringing the surface to an acceptable condition.

Sanding

Sanding should only be regarded as a final process before staining and polishing. Too often a power sander is used for processes that should have been done with a cutting tool. Sanding does not always remove wood. Fibers may be turned over instead of being rubbed off by excessive sanding. Sanding is an important final process, but the other steps should be done properly first.

The word *sanding* is a carryover from the days when abrasive paper was coated with sand. It is now coated with powdered glass, garnet, and many other types of manufactured abrasive grits. The backing may be paper or cloth. Older adhesives were not immune to dampness or sometimes to heat. so they would give up and the grit would be wasted. Modern abrasive cloths and papers have very tough adhesives. so the grits have longer lives.

Hand sanding is done with paper used loose in the hand or wrapped around a block. A piece of scrap wood may be suitable. but there are cork and rubber sanding blocks that give a little resilience. which is valuable. Although power sanding may be used. a final hand sanding is employed when the best possible finish is required.

Sanders

A power *orbital* sander takes flat sanding paper similar to that used for hand sanding (Fig. 5-11A). It is clipped to a backing pad. and the motor. which may be an electric drill, gives it a very rapid vibration over a small orbit. This can take the place of hand sanding for finishing, but it cannot be expected to sand away much wood.

A *disk* sander holds a circle of abrasive paper against a hard rubber disk mounted in an electric drill chuck (Fig. 5-11B). Such a tool is not of much use for finishing a surface, as it leaves a series of curved scratches. It is more useful at places like multiple joints, where pieces come from several

Fig. 5-11. An orbital sander (A) gives the smoothest results, but a sanding disk (B) will more quickly remove wood. A belt sander (C) also works quickly, without making the unwanted curved scratches a disk does.

directions and have to be leveled. It may also be used on rounded parts. particularly where there is end grain.

The power tool for in-line sanding is a *belt* sander. The abrasive cloth is in the form of a wide belt that passes around rollers and over a pressure pad (Fig. 5-11C). In one form the tool has handles and is moved over the wood like a plane. Alternatively the sander may be static and the wood moved over it.

A mishandled orbital sander is unlikely to do any damage, but it is all too easy for disk and belt sanders to mar a surface if used in unskilled hands. They are all right for coarse sanding. but finishing is often better completed by hand.

Power sanding can produce a lot of dust. Belt sanders usually have extractors to take away most of the dust; but if much power sanding is done. there should be good ventilation, and the wearing of a mask is advisable.

Making Holes

The portable electric drill is now the primary means of making holes, and it is often the first power tool in a tool kit. However, there are occasions when other means of making holes are preferable.

BRACE

The traditional tool for making holes in wood is a carpenter's brace (Fig. 6-1A). One of these incorporating a ratchet should be in the kit of anyone expecting to do much furniture repair or construction. Bits fit in the brace with a square-tapered shank (Fig. 6-1B). This gives a postive, nonslip drive, which is sometimes difficult to obtain when a large-diameter bit on a round shaft is fitted to the self-centering chuck of an electric drill.

BITS

The simplest center bits (Fig. 6-1C) make clean holes in thin material. If holes are to go deeper, they can be kept true by a twist bit. There are several forms, but the Irwin bit (Fig. 6-1D) is an example. The screw point pulls the bit in, and your energy is only needed to turn the brace.

Fig. 6-1. For making larger holes by hand, the brace (A) is the best tool. For deep holes the bit should be parallel (B), but for shallow holes the spade bit (C) is simpler. A screw point pulls the bit into the wood and reduces the need for heavy pressure on the brace (D).

Another use of the brace is as a screwdriver. A screwdriver bit in the chuck stands the best chance of moving a stubborn screw. either in or out. There is no other way of obtaining so much torque while maintaining enough pressure to hold the tool in place.

A brace is also the best tool for countersinking. A power drill. even a multispeed one on its slowest speed. really turns too fast for countersinking properly. This is even more so when countersinking metal. If a hinge needs the screws set in deeper. the slow turning of the brace gives better control, and the countersink bit actually cuts better.

For large holes an expanding brace-bit is likely to produce a better and cleaner hole than any of the devices used in power drills. Such a bit has an adjustable cutting edge that can be set to cut different diameters (Fig. 6-2). The bit is usually supplied with two adjustable pieces to cut up to about a 3 in. diameter.

ELECTRIC DRILLS

A difficulty. sometimes. with an electric drill is restraining it. If a small hole has to be drilled only a short

Fig. 6-2. The cutting end of an expanding bit. The cutter can be exchanged for the other cutter (left for smaller holes.)

distance to take the point of a screw. it is easy to go too deep or wobble the drill and make the hole too big. In this case. it is probably better to use a small wheel brace. which is much easier to control (Fig. 6-3A).

However. for small holes there is a *bradawl* (Fig. 6-3B)—a tool so simple that it is sharpened to a chisel edge. It is entered

Fig. 6-3. Small holes can be made with metalworking drills in a wheel brace (A) holes for small screws may be made with a bradawl (B).

across the grain and given half turns in each directions as it is pushed in. It does not remove wood. Because of this a screw is likely to have a better grip than if the usual drill had been used to remove wood.

For woodwork, particularly if wood-boring bits of diameter larger than the chuck capacity are to be used, an electric drill should be adjustable for slow speeds. Cuts are then easier to control and hole edges are made cleaner. When holes go right through, take the drill into scrap wood on the far side, or preferably stop when the point shows through, then drill back from the other side.

Metalworking drills up to about ¼ in. are satisfactory for holes in wood, although they tear the fibers and do not leave clean edges. For sizes larger than this there are adapations of the same form of drill with spurs and a center point (Fig. 6-4A. They will make straight, clean holes to their full length.

Above this size there are spade bits (Fig. 6-4B), with a form that would be unsuccessful in the slow-turning carpenter's brace. But at higher speeds they make good holes, although they may wander if taken too deep.

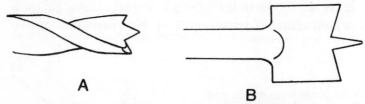

A   B

Fig. 6-4. For power drilling, bits can have relatively simple points.

For much larger holes there are hole saws and other devices that use cutters like sections of hacksaw blade or cutters that can be moved in or out, but these may not be as satisfactory as an expanding bit in a brace.

For much woodwork the electric drill is used freehand. However, accuracy depends on the eye. This also applies to using a brace. The operator can see the direction the drill is going from one way, but it is worthwhile having someone elso viewing from about a right angle to the operator's view as well. For accurate centering, it is advisable to make a dent for the start of the drill, even if the location is shown by two crossing pencil lines. A pointed awl can be used, or a center punch similar to that used for marking metal for drilling but with the point ground finer (about 30°).

Where greater precision is needed, as when drilling dowel holes that have to be square to the surface, it is a help to have the electric drill in a stand, preferably a heavy one (Fig. 6-5)

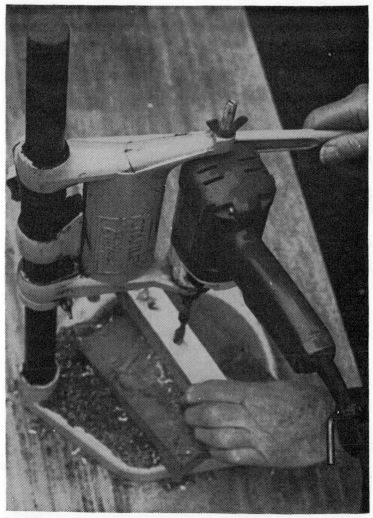

Fig. 6-5. Using an electric drill mounted in a stand. The assembly moves up and down the pillar and is controlled by the lever. A collar on the pillar controls depth.

rather than the light one sometimes offered for amateur use. This is also suitable for use with attachments for drilling a series of holes to remove the waste in a mortise accurately. With the stop usually provided on the column of the stand, it is possible to control the depth of drilling precisely, which is important in such jobs as getting a series of turned posts set in equally or avoiding screw holes going too far and breaking through the other side.

DEEP AND LARGE HOLES

If holes have to be taken very deep—as when putting an electric wire through a lamp standard—there is often a difficulty in keeping any drilling device straight, because wood is a natural material, and wanderings and variations of hardness in the grain may deflect the bit. It is sometimes possible to make the piece in two parts or cut the wood to be used down the center. The hole is then made by grooving the two halves and gluing them together. With the strength of glues available today, the properly assembled parts should be at least as strong as the solid wood.

Long holes may be started with normal drills, with great care to obtain straightness, preferably using the electric drill in a stand for greatest precision. If the hole is to go through, it can be started from both ends. The tool for going deeper is an *auger*. This is a long twist bit, with a socket for a handle at the end instead of a shank to fit a brace (Fig. 6-6). With the first hole as a guide, this should work its way through without

Fig. 6-6. An auger is an older means of drilling.

straying. The auger should be withdrawn occasionally to clear waste; otherwise this can build up, and in wood of thin section, it could exert enough pressure to cause the wood to burst. In some woods it may be a help in reducing friction to grease the twisted part with candle fat, but do not use ordinary oil.

There are special augers supplied for use in some lathes for turning long standards that have to be bored. A long auger to be used in a brace can be made by welding an extension on an ordinary woodworking twist bit.

When holes larger than those that can be made with any expanding bit are needed, it is possible to saw them, but it is very difficult to get a true circle with a clean edge. A power router may have an arrangement for allowing it to travel in a circular path, possibly by using a spike or nail through a hole in its adjustable fence. This can be used to make a true circle with a clean edge. Of course, it is limited in depth. Most cutters will cut through about ½ in.

If the wood is thicker, go as deep as the cutter will go, then remove the rest of the waste with a jigsaw or other saw and carefully work the edge of the circle with gouges or a Surform tool. This will look better than a circle made completely by through and the router used on the back as well, but only a slight discrepance will put the two cut circles a little out of line.

Fastenings

In the best furniture construction most joints are fitted and glued and have no metal fastenings. Where metal fastenings are needed, these are screws rather than nails, except in places that will not be seen. In less important furniture there may be more use of screws, nails, and other metal fastenings.

Many modern glues have such strong adhesion that they can be relied on even in places where they do not have the benefit of cut joints to relieve the glue of some of the direct load. With some glues the joint may be stronger than the wood, so wood fibers give way before the glue line in a test to destruction.

GLUES

Until World War II the common woodworking glue was made from bones, hooves, and other animal products. There were liquid glues in cans and tubes, but most glue was heated for use. It had adequate strength, as shown by the many old pieces of furniture still in sound condition; but this type of glue weakened to the point of becoming useless in damp conditions and would also soften if it became hot. Animal glue is obsolescent, but it might be needed to match existing glue in restoration work. It is not compatible with modern glues, so any remaining in a failed joint should be scraped away before using another glue.

Another glue that dates from before World War II and is still in use is casein (*Casco* in one trade name). This is derived from milk. It is usually supplied as a white powder to mix with water into a paste. It has reasonable strength and some resistance to dampness, but immersion will soften it (although strength might return when it dries out). Casein still has uses for large laminations and other constructional woodwork inside buildings, but for furniture construction the craftsman in the home shop will find other glues more useful.

Synthetic Resins

Most woodworking glues are synthetic resins. As they are often known only by trade names, it is not always easy to identify them. Careful reading of the description or instructions will give a clue to the type. If an adhesive is described as being suitable for fabric, paper, and other things besides wood, it is unlikely to have the maximum strength needed for joints in furniture construction, although it may be quite satisfactory for light decorative work or toys. If the glue is in two parts, that is a sign that it is a strong, waterproof one. If it is a one-part glue and the information on the container only mentions wood, it is also likely to be a good glue for furniture joints, although it might not be a good choice for anything that will be exposed to rain.

One of the powerful synthetic resin glues is resorcinol. Its glue line is a reddish-brown color, which makes it undesirable on some woods. It is used in plywood and some commercial production, but it needs a close-fitting joint and must be clamped tightly. It does not bond to the resins used with fiberglass, so it may be unsuitable for furniture that combines wood and fiberglass. Although it may have some uses in the home shop, there are other glues more generally useful.

A good, general-purpose two-part synthetic resin is based on urea. It is not so fully waterproof that it will withstand very prolonged immersion, but otherwise, once it has set it will retain a strength at least as great as the wood in any conditions furniture is likely to meet. In one form the glue is a syrup with a shelf life of a few months. Alternatively, it may be a long-life powder to mix with water to maks the syrup. With this there is a catalyst (hardener), which is a mild acid. When catalyst and syrup are brought together, a chemical reaction drives out the water and the glue sets permanently. The process cannot be reversed. The catalyst may be mixed with the syrup before use; then the mixture must be used in the time specified by the maker (20 minutes is typical). Alternatively the syrup may go on one surface and the catalyst on the other so that reaction does not start until they are brought together. In another form both catalyst and glue are in powder form and may be together in one container. So long as the powder mixture is dry, the glue has a long storage life; but when water is added, reaction commences and the glue has to be used in the time indicated on the container.

Urea glue is best used with a reasonably close joint, but this is not as critical as with resorcinol. Great pressure is not needed—clamping need only be enough to maintain a close contact. Setting time varies according to the catalyst and temperature. In most cases the joint may be handled and worked within a few hours, but strength continues to build up, probably over several days or weeks. Urea glue may be used with wood and fiberglass.

There are glues with bases other than urea. If in two parts, they may be assumed to be at least as strong as urea. The glue with the greatest strength and versatility is based on epoxy, but it is expensive and so is not usually chosen when another glue will do. It is a two-part glue that not only joins wood to wood but will join almost any material, including metal, to the same or some other material. Most synthetic glues have to be used above certain minimum temperatures (normal room or shop temperature is satisfactory), but epoxy can be used close to freezing.

Using Glue

Some woods will discolor if the glue parts are mixed in a metal container or applied with a metal-bound brush. Mixing in a throwaway plastic container and applying with a piece of wood is better. Mix glue and catalyst by hand. A power mixer

71

may introduce too many air bubbles. If any joint is too open or there is a part to be built up, sawdust can be mixed with the glue until it has the consistency of putty. This can be pressed or molded to shape and will have a strength comparable to the plain glue. If plain glue is used in bulk, it will craze as it sets and will have no strength. With sawdust the glue is employed bonding the tiny particles of wood, and it does not craze. Using this mixture instead of Plastic Wood or other filler provides strength, but a filler would only provide shape.

SCREWS

Wood screws are described by their length from the surface of the wood, their thickness by gauge number, the type of head, and the material. There is no easier way of familiarizing oneself with screw sizes than by examining a selection, since the gauge numbers do not represent sizes easily visualized. Except in the smaller sizes, the even-number gauges are more easily obtained than the odd-number ones. Some generally useful sizes are ½ in. by 4, ¾ in. by 6, 1 in. by 8, and 1½ in. by 10; but all lengths may be had thicker or thinner.

Unless there is a need for something else, flat-head screws are commonly used (Fig. 7-1A). Round-head screws (Fig. 7-1B) are not often used directly with wood, but they are suitable for some metal fittings. The oval head (Fig. 7-1C) also

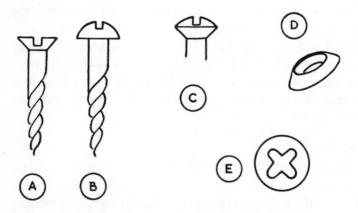

Fig. 7-1. The variety of heads screws can have.

looks well where the screw head is visible on a fitting. If a panel has to be removed occasionally, oval-head screws through cup washers (Fig. 7-1D) make a good choice.

General-purpose screws have straight slots, but Phillips and other comparable screws have star-shaped recesses (Fig. 7-1E). These are intended to prevent slippage with power screwdrivers in production work, but there are hand screwdrivers to fit.

Most screws are bright steel. There is a risk of rusting, not only from dampness in the air but from chemicals in some wood; so in the best cabinetwork it is usual to have brass screws, which are less likely to corrode. A rusted steel screw in some oak may seize so it cannot be withdrawn, and it will eventually corrode to the breaking point. Stainless steel, bronze, and other metals, and some plastics, are used for screws for special purposes, and most metal screws may be obtained plated to match the finish of the fittings they pass through.

Except for the smallest screws in softer woods, it is important to drill first. A screw usually has to pull two pieces together by squeezing the upper part between the screw head and the lower part gripped by the thread. Consequently there should be a clearance hole through the top piece (Fig. 7-2A). If the plain shank of the screw will continue into the lower piece, the clearance hole should go that far as well. There is no fixed size of lower hole for each screw, as the type of wood affects it. A small screw that does not have to go far in a softwood may cut its own way in, or a bradawl hole may be sufficient.

In harder woods the hole should be made about the same as the core diameter of the thread. The screw can be left to cut its own way for perhaps two threads (Fig. 7-2B) in many woods, or the hole may have to go the full depth in really hard woods.

A flat head will pull in flush in softwoods and some plywood. Hardwoods will require use of a countersink bit, but even then there will be slight pull-in, so be careful not to countersink too much.

Screwdrivers should have ends which make a reasonably close fit in the screw head. This means having several

Fig. 7-2. Holes should be drilled to clear the screw shank (A) and be the tapping size for the threaded part (B).

screwdrivers. A long screwdriver is easier to use than a short one. but in furniture construction there are often places where a long screwdriver will not go. A collection of plain screwdrivers is worth having. Additionally there may be

Fig. 7-3. Screwdrivers. The long one has a pump action and can be adjusted to drive or withdraw screws, or it can be used as a ratchet only. Its chuck takes several bit sizes. In front of it is a plain screwdriver with a plastic handle and one with a traditional wooden handle. The fluted-handle driver has a point for Phillips head screws; the steel screwdriver with wood cheeks is more of an engineer's tool. To the right is a screwdriver bit to fit a brace, it is useful when considerable leverage is needed to turn a screw.

ratchet and pump-action (Yankee) types with various points (Fig. 7-3). A pump-action screwdriver may also take small bits for making the screw holes.

Sometimes the screw heads must be hidden. In this case the screws can be counterbored to put the heads below the surface. A hole is drilled larger than the screw head, and this is plugged after the screw has been tightened (Fig. 7-4). For the best effect the plug is cut cross-grained from a piece of wood that matches that being fastened. This can be made with a plug cutter, which is like a hollow bit used in an electric drill stand.

Fig. 7-4. A screw head can be sunk below the surface of a piece of furniture and concealed with a plug.

Keep the ends of screwdrivers filed or ground so they do not have rounded corners or edges. A worn screwdriver or one of the wrong size may jump off the screw and mar the adjoining wood.

NAILS AND TOOLS FOR NAILING

Nails are described by their length. Although they are made to gauge thicknesses, there is usually little choice, and the thickness usual for a particular length will have to be accepted. There is a system of *penny* sizes for nails—2d. is 1 in. long. 60d. is 6 in. long. It is probably better to avoid this system and order nails by length.

There is a very large range of nails available, mostly for purposes other than furniture making. Common box nails have flat heads (Fig. 7-5A). These are usually bright steel. The head gives a safe grip. particularly for a piece of thin plywood at the back of a cabinet or similar construction. There are different sizes of heads. but none is likely to be acceptable on a finished exposed surface.

Nails may be bronzed or otherwise treated to improve their appearance. There are brass, copper, aluminum, and other metal nails, but some of them are inclined to bend or buckle if holes are not drilled.

Some nails are obtainable with ringed shanks. The rings give the nail something of the grip of a screw, but if it has to be withdrawn, it will tear up the surrounding surface.

If nails are to be used in a place where the surface is visible, there are nails with only slight heads. Larger ones are *casing* nails and finer ones are *finishing* nails (Fig. 7-5B). These can be driven below the surface with a nail punch (Fig. 7-5C) then the head can be covered with stopping. In good furniture, nailing is to be kept to a minimum, but sometimes

Fig. 7-5. Box nails (A) can't be easily concealed, but a casing nail (B) can be driven below the surface with a punch (C) and covered with stopping.

molding or a decorative piece has to be fixed in this way. The strips holding glass in a cabinet door may also be nailed. If furniture is to be fixed to a masonry wall and nails are used instead of screws in plugs, there are hardened-steel masonry nails which can be used. Screws are preferable to nails for most furniture construction.

Nails in general carpentry are usually driven without any predrilling, but in the hardwoods and sometimes in narrow sections used for furniture, it is often advisable to drill for nails, particularly if the nail is to come near an edge. The hole in the upper piece may be just slightly undersize, while the one in the lower part may be about half the nail diameter and not taken the full depth. Much depends on the wood.

If a nail bends when being driven, it is usually wiser to withdraw it and use another than to straighten it and continue. Pincers or a claw hammer will remove the nail, but be careful that surrounding wood is not damaged in the process. Put a piece of thin wood where the pincers will lever.

The spacing of nails or screws is a matter of experience. When covering a framework with plywood, spacing around the edges should be closer than fastenings driven into intermediate frames, and at the edges it may be advisable to have a few closer fastenings near the corners. Nails driven

Fig. 7-6. Driving nails at opposing angles makes strong joints (A). A hammer with a narrow cross peen (B) is useful for fine nails.

alternately at opposite angles (Fig. 7-6A) in dovetail fashion will have an increased grip.

Almost any hammer will drive nails, but if one is bought for furniture work, it is useful to have a cross peen (Fig. 7-6B), which will go between finger and thumb when holding a small nail or hit in a recess that will not admit the flat peen. Nails in awkward places are best driven with the aid of a punch. For the pinlike nails often used in cabinetwork, a very light hammer (about 4 oz) is best.

Glued And Lapped Joints

Joints in woodwork provide strength by the overlapping and interlocking of parts. Sometimes the joint produces strength by the combination of grains in different directions.

Glue grips best on the side of the grain. The grip directly on end grain may be very slight, so joints are designed to bring meeting surfaces together either with the grain or at a shallow angle to it. Wood joints are made to give good glue area for maximum adhesion. The only joints that are not glued are those which use wedges or keys, as in some garden furniture and traditional pieces and in those items which may have to be dismantled.

MAKING PANELS

The width of a board obviously cannot be more than the thickness of the tree from which it was cut. At one time much furniture making involved the building up of boards to width, and some paneled furniture of earlier days was designed that way as much to avoid wide boards as for the sake of appearance. With plywood and the many other forms of manufactured builtup boards, many of the problems of wide panels can be avoided. The range of sheet material with veneers and other surface finishes is such that pieces up to any usual furniture width can be found to match the solid wood elsewhere in the piece. For new work these wide materials are usually chosen, but there are many places, even in new construction, where edge-to-edge joints have to be made, and there are several points to watch.

It is inadvisable to glue two machine-planed edges without other preparation. The action of machine planing, particularly if the cutters are not perfectly sharp, "casehardens" the surface so that it resists the penetration of glue. The edges should be hand-planed—not sanded. Any form of sanding tends to round the angles, and this is undesirable. Difficulty in these joints often comes at the ends, where the pieces may tend to spring apart and open the joint. This can be obviated by planing the edges very slightly hollow. A bar clamp across the middle will then pull the whole joint close (Fig. 8-1A). *Joiner's dogs* are also useful for pulling ends close (Fig. 8-1B).

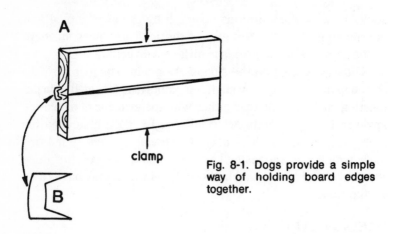

clamp

Fig. 8-1. Dogs provide a simple way of holding board edges together.

Their inner tapered legs give a wedge action as they are driven (Fig. 8-2).

If wood warps, the tendency is for annual rings to straighten. If several boards are to be joined to make up a width, it is good practice to examine the ends and arrange the curves of annual rings in alternate directions (Fig. 8-3). Little warping may be expected from properly seasoned furniture

Fig. 8-2. A dog is driven into the end grain of two boards to draw their glued edges together. Note that the points are sedges with their bevels inwards.

woods. but if it does occur. overall distortion will be minimized.

A system called *secret slot screwing* can be used to pull glued edges together without clamps and impart some cross-grain strength. This is particularly useful when a very long joint is being made. as the screws also keep the boards in the same plane. Screws driven into one board have to mate with slots in the other. How many are used along a joint depends on the wood and its thickness. but a spacing of 6 in. in softwood 1 in. thick. or 12 in. in hardwood. is reasonable.

The centers are marked on both pieces. then the piece which will not have the screws driven into it has additional marks made. two to three times the diameter of the screw head from the first. Screws are driven until the threads are buried. In the opposite piece there is a hole to clear the screw head. taken a little deeper than the screw projects. and a slot

Fig. 8-3. Having grain opposite ways reduces the risk of overall warping.

alongside it wide enough to clear the shank of the screw (Fig. 8-4A).

The boards are brought together dry, and the screws are inserted in their opposite holes; then one board is driven along the other so the screw heads cut along the grain (Fig. 8-4B). If this test assembly is satisfactory, the joint is knocked apart and the screws each are given a quarter turn. Glue is applied and the joints driven together again.

Another way of strengthening and securing a glued joint is to have dowels across it at intervals (Fig. 8-4C). The dowels should be about one-third the thickness of the wood. Careful marking and straight drilling will make a good joint. If possible, drill with an electric drill in a stand. There can be a bursting action when a dowel goes into its hole like a piston into a cylinder if air and surplus glue cannot escape. Making a saw cut along the dowel gives a safety groove.

Fig. 8-4. "Secret" slot screws (A and B) are an old cabinetmaker's way of pulling edges tight. Dowels (C) provide strength across the grain in a joint.

LAP JOINTS

When two pieces of wood have to cross or meet and the surfaces have to be flush, the simplest joint is a *lap* joint. There are many variations. In the basic cross lap (Fig. 8-5A) both parts are the same size. The same joint may be a corner or end lap (Fig. 8-5B), or a middle lap (Fig. 8-5C) at a T-junction. The parts are not always the same width or thickness, or flush, or at a right angle.

In general it is inadvisable to cut away more than half the thickness of the thinner part. The parts to be joined should be marked from the face surfaces and the widths of cuts should be obtained from the actual pieces (Fig. 8-5D). Use a marking gauge from the face side on both pieces. All other lines are best made with a knife so as to sever the fibers and allow a clean cut with the saw. Mark the waste parts to prevent mistakes. Saw cuts have to be made on the waste sides of the lines. It is a help, in preventing the saw carrying its kerf over the line, to bevel on the waste side of the knife-cut line with a chisel (Fig. 8-5E) as a guide for the start of the saw cut.

Fig. 8-5. Lap joints: cross lap (A), corner or end lap (B), middle lap (C). The widths of the cuts are taken from the pieces (D); the one to be inset is beveled with a chisel (E).

Making the Cut

With the wood in the vise or against the bench hook, use a fine backsaw. To avoid going too deep, the saw can be tilted forward until down to the line on the far side, then back until the near side is reached. Finally a few light strokes are made horizontally until the depth is the same right through. In many cases no other sawing is needed; but if the wood is very wide, intermediate cuts can be made in the waste part to ease its removal by chiseling. Although a small circular saw would have the benefit of controlling the depth of cut, it is difficult to get it exactly on the line for a precision cut, so it is usually better to make lap joints by hand.

With the wood in the vise use a board chisel to pare diagonally into the joint (Fig. 8-6). Go very close to the gauge line, then turn the wood around and do the same from the other

Fig. 8-6. Using a chisel to pare diogonally into a joint.

side. Finally pare straight across. Check that the bottom of the cut is level. A slight hollowing tendency is less of a fault than for the bottom to be higher in the middle.

Where one part is the end of a piece of wood, it can be sawn completely. Marking is the same as for a cross lap, but it is advisable to leave a little extra on the end to be planed after assembly (Fig. 8-7A).

After making the cross-grained cut, hold the wood in the vise at a slight angle. Saw diagonally on the waste side of the gauge line, watching progress of the kerf across the end and down the side (Fig. 8-7B). Turn the wood over and do the same the other way (Fig. 8-7C), and then cut straight through (Fig. 8-7D). After a little practice a satisfactory result will be obtained simply from the saw; but if necessary, the meeting surface can be trimmed with a chisel.

This cut can be made on a table saw, providing the wood is not so long as to be unwieldy and the depth of cut is no more

Fig. 8-7. Cutting joint parts with a backsaw.

than the projection of the saw blade. The wood is traversed over the saw at the right depth setting, against the fence set to the final thickness. In the usual right-angled joint, the wood has to be kept upright, and a push piece with a square corner is helpful (Fig. 8-8).

Fig. 8-8. Parts for a right-angled joint must be kept upright when they are being cut on a table saw.

The tool techniques involved in making lap joints occur in many other joints, so lap or halving construction forms a good introduction to the making of other joints.

Variations of Lap Joint

Some variations of the simple lap joint inclued a *stopped* lap joint, where it would spoil the appearance of an edge if the

85

Fig. 8-9. A stopped lap joint (A) may be needed in some circumstances. A miter (B) looks bettter on the surface. A dovetail, either on one or both sides of the joint (C and D) resists pull on the crosspiece. A halving joint (E) is useful for partitons in a box.

end grain of the T-piece showed through (Fig. 8-9A). If a corner would lock better with a miter showing on the face side, the *halving* joint can be adopted (Fig. 8-9B) but this is not as strong as a full lap joint. If the load taken may tend to pull on the joint, this can be resisted by using a *dovetail* form for either one (Fig. 8-9C) or both (Fig. 8-9D) sides of the joint. This can be combined with a stopped lap joint. A halving joint can be made edgewise on the wood (Fig. 8-9E); this is useful for partitions in a box.

Tenon And Dowel Joints

9

The greatest integral strength, as distinct from any strength glue may contribute, comes in joints in which one part fits into another rather than resting on it or being recessed into a side. There are many places where other joints are more appropriate, but the joints most used in furniture of framed construction are those in which a piece projecting from one part fits into a socket in another piece. When the projecting piece is part of the solid wood, it is a *tenon*, and the socket it fits into is a *mortise*. Although dowels had some use in traditional furniture, they get much greater use today, as power tools make them easier to use with accuracy for joints that would otherwise have been tenoned.

MORTISE-AND-TENON JOINTS

In the basic mortise-and-tenon joint between two pieces at right angles (Fig. 9-1), it is usual for the tenon to be about one-third of the width of the wood on which it is cut. This applies when the other piece is the same or a similar width. If the other piece is much wider, there will be greater strength if the tenoned piece is not cut away as much. Although it is unusual to chop out mortises completely with a chisel, a chisel will have to be used for trimming. It is a help to make the tenon

Fig. 9-1. The basic elements of a mortise-and-tenon joint.

and mortise to match a chisel rather than a measurement obtained from a rule.

Allow a little extra on the end of the tenoned piece if it is to go right through; it can be planed flush later. Cut around the shoulders with a knife and use a mortise gauge to mark the tenon (Fig. 9-2A). On the other piece, mark the mortise limits with pencil and carry them around to the other side with a try square down the face surface. Mark the width of the mortise on both sides with the gauge (Fig. 9-2B). Saw away the waste on each side of the tenon as described for a sawn lap joint (Figs. 8-7 and 8-8).

Fig. 9-2. In its simplest form the mortise-and-tenon joint is one-third the thickness of the pieces joined.

To make the mortise with a chisel only, the wood is supported on the bench (not in the vise, where grain on the far side might break out). Then a chisel of the same width as the mortise is used with a mallet to chop centrally and make further cuts towards the ends, but not right up to them at first (Fig. 9-3A). The same chisel, or a narrower one, is used to hook out the waste, and the process is repeated, if necessary, until the cut reaches halfway. Then the wood is turned over and the same is done from the other side. Finally, the chisel pares down to the line at each end of the mortise. Such a joint is clamped and glued.

It is more usual to use an electric drill, used freehand or in a stand, to remove most of the waste. It is possible to use a slightly undersize drill to make holes which just touch the mortise edges and leave little wood to be removed with a chisel (Fig. 9-3B). Another method uses a guide for the drill, which is fed into intermediate positions between the first row of holes and leaves extremely little waste to be removed. If the strip of wood can be moved along a guide piece, the drill itself can remove the remaining waste, leaving only the ends of the mortise to be squared with a chisel (Fig. 9-3C).

Fig. 9-3. A mortise-and-tenon joint may be chopped out (A). Overlapping drilled holes will remove most of the waste (B and C).

Another way is to use a router, which enters the wood and then moves sideways to cut the slot. To do this accurately, the wood must be locked in a slide which traverses the wood correctly in relation to the cutter. Professional mortising is often done with a special hollow chisel. This is square and sharpened on the inside. An auger turns in its center. This combination is lowered into the wood, and the chisel pares downward as the auger removes waste (Fig. 9-4A). The mortise is made by working a series of squares. There are accessories for some electric drills which allow this method to be used in a home shop.

In some constructions a dowel may be put through the joint. This is valuable in a place where clamping is difficult or impossible. The hole in the tenon is staggered slightly from that in the mortised piece so that driving in a dowel with a tapered end pulls the joint together (Fig. 9-4B). In some traditional and any takedown furniture, the tenon is made long enough to leave a tusk to take a wedge or key (Fig. 9-4C) which pulls the joint tight and holds it.

Fig. 9-4. A special hollow tool can be used in a power drill (A) to remove the waste in a mortise made with overlapping holes. A peg through staggered holes (B) will pull a tenon into its mortise. Wedges through extended tenons (C) are found in some traditional furniture.

Other Mortise-and-Tenon Joints

If the tenon would be unsightly if taken right through, as in a rail to a leg, a *stub (blind)* tenon is used (Fig. 9-5A). There is no difficulty in making this joint except in getting the depth of the mortise right. Ideally the tenon should touch bottom as the shoulders meet the surface, but since it is more important for appearance that the shoulders be tight, it is usual to cut the mortise a little deeper.

It is possible to make this joint extra firm by *fox-wedging*: The inside of the mortise tapers outward slightly at the ends, then wedges in saw cuts in the tenon spread it as it is driven home (Fig. 9-5B). Wedges are sometimes used with through tenons, but this is more common in doors and house construction than in furniture making.

Fig. 9-5. Variations on the mortise-and-tenon joint include one that uses a stub, or blind, tenon (A) and one made extra secure by fox wedging (B).

If two rails meet in a log, the ends can be mitered to allow the maximum lengths of tenons (Fig. 9-6A). If one surface of the tenoned piece is to come level with the surface of the other piece, it can be *barefaced* (Fig. 9-6B). This is also useful for a rail which is not very thick. A shoulder cut in both sides might leave little strength in the remaining wood in the tenon. There is a secondary advantage in having only one shoulder to cut: This will pull close, but if two shoulders are not cut exactly the same, one side may not be as good a fit as the other.

When the joint comes at a corner, it may be an open or *bridle* joint (Fig. 9-6C). Although this may have some uses in

Fig. 9-6. Tenons on rails can be made to meet within the joint by mitering their ends (A); the barefaced tenon is often used on rails that aren't very thick. Corners may show parts (C), or be stopped (D and E).

carpentry, it is uncommon in furniture construction. It is more usual to cut the tenon back to make a *haunched* mortise-and-tenon joint (Fig. 9-6D). The tapered haunch does not show at the end. It is usual to leave some waste on the end of the mortised piece and not remove this until after the joint had been glued. Doing so reduces any risk of the end grain breaking out as the mortise is cut or the joint assembled. If the framing includes a panel recessed into grooves, the tenon is cut back to the bottom of the groove, and the haunch may be squared to fit the groove in the other piece (Fig. 9-6E).

Special Large Joints

If the piece to be tenoned is very wide, the mortise to take a large single tenon might weaken the mortised piece. In that case there can be two parts to the tenon, with or without a short piece between (Fig. 9-7A). If the tenoned part is very thick, two tenons (Fig. 9-7B) may be better than a single thick one. If quite wide boards are to be joined, there can be a large number of pins, with spaces of about the same width as the pins. If the pins have diagonal saw cuts made in them before assembly, they can be tightened with glued wedges (Fig. 9-7C).

If mortise-and-tenon joints are not at right angles, they should be designed so shaping the tenons does not cut across lines of grain, even if this means entering at an angle (Fig. 9-7D). Breaking through grain weakens the wood.

The mortise-and-tenon principle can be adapted to many types of assembly. For instance, a piece tenoned into another with a rabbet can have long and short shoulders (Fig. 9-7E), which will look better than if we cut away the other part to allow both shoulders to be in the same plane.

Fig. 9-7. Where the wood is wide or shaped, you can use the special joints shown.

DOWELING

Old craftsmen made dowels as they needed them. Today it is more usual to buy machine-made dowel rods in various woods and in many lengths and diameters. Not all wood is suitable for manufacture in this way, so if a particular wood is needed, the craftsman may still make his own. Some oak furniture looks well with the ends of dowels exposed at joints. These should be oak, but it is unlikely that ready-made lengths can be bought.

Dowels can be made on a lathe, but they are more readily made with a *dowel plate* (Fig. 9-8A), which is merely a stout drilled steel plate, used over a vise or mounted on a block of wood. The holes may taper, but plain drilled ones will work. This wood is planed square, then the corners planed off. A rough taper is chiseled on one end, then the stick is driven through the plate. Dowels are best made this way only slightly longer than the length needed for one dowel.

Dowels, whether homemade or cut from a length, should be tapered slightly at the ends, and it is an advantage to groove along them with a saw (Fig. 9-8B) to allow air and excess glue

Fig. 9-8. Dowels can be made by knocking wood through holes in a plate (A). A groove along a dowel allows air and surplus glue to escape (B).

to escape. The main problem in doweling is obtaining squareness in mating pieces. The use of an electric drill in a stand helps, but not all assemblies can be held this way. There are doweling jigs which clamp to the wood and guide the drill squarely to the surface. If much doweling is to be done, such a jig is essential for consistently good work.

If drilling has to be done without any mechanical aid to control direction, the wood should be secured against movement. and a hollow should be made where the drill is to enter. either with a spike or a punch. It is useful to have an assistant to view the drill. but if you are working along. standing one or more try squares nearby gives something to check by.

Some doweling jigs help in spacing dowel holes on the parts to be joined. In any case there has to be accurate marking of holes. The need for this becomes more acute as the number of dowels in a joint increases. one slightly incorrect dowel being enough to prevent assembly. In some joints it is possible to use a template on both pieces (Fig. 9-9) or make a jig with pointed nails to mark both surfaces.

Fig. 9-9. A template can be used to mark the positions for dowels in a joint.

There is no standard way of deciding on the size and spacing of dowels; it depends on experience. Diameters should not usually be as much as half the thickness of the wood. and the space between the edges of holes is usually greater than the dowel diameter. To keep parts correctly registered in relation to each other. there should be at least two dowels in a joint (Fig. 9-10A).

Dowels do not usually go right through. The amount of projection in a framed structure might be about three-quarters of the thickness of the wood. It is usual to go about the same distance into each piece (Fig. 9-10B).

It is sometimes advisable to drill for dowels before other work has been finished. If two rabbeted parts are to join and dowels are to be used instead of a tenon (Fig. 9-10C). drilling the holes before the rabbets are made is easy; atferwards it would be almost impossible to do accurately.

Dowels stengthen joints where end grains meet and glue would not provide a good grip, yet an elaborate joint is not

Fig. 9-10. At least two dowels are needed to keep joint parts properly aligned (A); they should project into the mating parts by the same amount (B). When dowels are used instead of a tenon in a joint with a rabbet, the holes for them should be drilled before the rabbet is cut (C).

justified. A mitered corner between pieces that add decoration more than strength on the top of a high cabinet is an example (Fig. 9-11A). The dowels must be at right angles to the surfaces that meet, unlike tenons, which have to follow grain lines.

Fig. 9-11. Dowels can help glue get a grip on the end grain of mitered corner pieces (A). They can also be used to provide a grip for a screw in end grain (B).

Screws do not hold well in end grain, but dowels can be used to provide extra grip (Fig. 9-11B). The dowel should be far enough down for there to be no risk of the end grain fracturing under the pull of the screw on the dowel, and the screw should be long enough to go almost through the dowel.

Dovetail Joints

10

If any one family of joints can be regarded as the mark of fine cabinetwork, it is the dovetail. With the tenon flared, there is a resistance in pulling apart in one direction, whether glue or metal fastenings are also used or not. The design of dovetails varies. Oldtime craftsmen were very proud of making the joints with extremely narrow pins between the dovetails (Fig. 10-1A). This was certainly a sign of their skill, but the joints could not have been as strong as if the pins had been made wider. At the other extreme are machine-made dovetails, which are quite satisfactory; but the pins and dovetails are the same width (Fig. 10-B). Hand-cut dovetails are probably best kept to sizes between the two extremes.

The taper ratio of the sides of the dovetails is usually about 1:8 (Fig. 10-1C). This suits most hardwoods. Softwoods might be broadened slightly, but the ratio should not be less than 1:6. A piece of thin sheet metal may be bent and filed for use as a template (Fig. 10-D).

THROUGH DOVETAILS

A through dovetail joint may be the single kind (Fig. 10-2A) or the multiple kind (Fig. 10-2B). It may take a little experimenting to get an even spacing. The joint may be cut by

Fig. 10-1. Dovetails are found in most traditional furniture and are con sidered the mark of good craftsmanship. Handmade dovetails have nar row pins (A), but machine made dovetails have parts of equal width (B). The taper ratio of dovetail sides is usually 1:8 (C); a piece of bent sheet metal serves as a guide to its shape (D).

hand, dovetails first or pins first. To cut the dovetail piece first, mount the wood in a vise and saw down the sides of the dovetail with a backsaw on the waste side of the lines (Fig. 10-2C). Chop out the remaining waste with a bevel-edged chisel, working a little from each side on the bench. Then use the chisel to pare back to the line.

With the other piece in the vise and the depth marked all around, the dovetail piece is put in position, and a fine pencil point or a sharp awl is used to mark the shapes on the end. Then these are squared down to the line (Fig. 10-2D). Be

Fig. 10-2. Through dovetails. Joints may be single or multiple (A and B). Much of the waste can be sawn from one part, then this can be used to mark the other part (C and D).

careful to saw on the waste side of the lines. Some of the waste can be removed by diagonal saw cuts. In large joints it may be advisable to drill a series of holes across the waste or use a scroll saw to cut most of it away. Final trimming is done with a chisel, but be careful of damaging the tapered sides of the pins. If cutting pins first is favored, marking one from the other is in a different sequence, but otherwise the cutting is the same.

A craftsman prefers not to make a trial assembly, although this may be desirable for a beginner. Check that the bottoms of the cuts are in line and flat across the thickness of the wood. A trial assembly tends to loosen the joint, so if you trust your judgment and workmanship, apply glue and make the first assembly the last.

CONCEALED JOINTS

In some furniture, exposed joints may be regarded as a desirable feature, but elsewhere it is better if the joints are concealed, at least in one direction. In a drawer, for example, the dovetails should not show on the front. This is accomplished by a *stopped* or *blind* dovetail joint (Fig. 10-3A).

The dovetails are marked and cut in the same way as for a through dovetail, but they are only long enough to go part way across the other piece. How far across depends on the total thickness, but there must be enough material left to resist breaking out during the chopping operation.

The depth is marked on the second piece, which is held in the vise while the dovetail shapes are drawn on it. A gauge line will ensure even depth. Not much can be sawn away, but a fine backsaw can be used to cut diagonally as far as possible on the waste side of each line, then some cuts can be made in the waste (Fig. 10-3B). The rest of the waste has to be removed by chisel, cutting across the grain before slicing along it (Fig. 10-3C). Have the wood supported on a bench top or other solid surface and be careful not to go too deep with the chisel.

The dovetails can be hidden in both directions if a *stopped lap* dovetail joint is used. A narrow edge still shows (Fig. 10-3D). One place where this is used is in the corner of a plinth under a cabinet. The pattern of the joint being marked may be throught of as a blind dovetail joint with a flap over the second layer of end grain. It is like a through dovetail with an extra thickness on the outside of both pieces to be joined.

Prepare the wood by cutting back the piece that is to overlap (Fig. 10-3E). It does not matter which piece carries the dovetails; it depends on which way the resistance to pull is to come in relation to the narrow piece of exposed end grain. Mark the thickness of the part of the other piece that is to be jointed on both pieces and outline and dovetails. Cut these as far as possible by sawing. Most of the work will be careful chopping and paring with a chisel. Mark the second piece from the first and cut it similarly.

Fig. 10-3. In drawers and similar constructions, dovetail joints are stopped so the construction is hidden in one direction.

Mitered Dovetail

The ultimate in hand dovetailing is a mitered dovetail, in which no sign of the joint is visible (Fig. 10-4A). This may be thought of as a through dovetail with an extra thickness on both pieces. Both parts are prepared by cutting back the amount that will be mitered. but it is safer not to plane or chisel the miters at this stage. It is difficult to keep the saw or chisel from going farther than intended when cutting the dovetails and pins. but this will not matter if it only goes into the waste that is yet to be removed (Fig. 10-4B). In some work it will not matter if the miter does not extend across the thickness of the wood. as this will be hidden; but if the edge will be exposed in the finished construction. allow for mitering the edges (Fig. 10-4C).

Fig. 10-4. In a mitered dovetail, construction is hidden.

Cutting is similar to that for stopped and lapped joints. When the dovetail parts are completed. the miter can be trimmed with a paring chisel. A shoulder plane is a good tool for final leveling.

Other Dovetail Joints

There are several devices for making dovetails by machine. For home use there is an arrangement which clamps the wood and acts as a template for a rotary router. which can be driven by an electric drill or other power source. The method gives automatic accuracy and spacing. usually with pins and dovetails the same width (Fig. 10-5A). The rounded ends may seem less satisfactory than squared corners. but in practice the joints are satisfactory.

If dovetailing is to be used where parts meet obliquely. the angles of the dovetails should be related to the lines of grain

(Fig. 10-5B) in the same way as mortise-and-tenon joints meet. If a drawer side is to be grooved for a plywood bottom, the bottom half-dovetail can be made wide enough to take the groove and hide it in the joint (Fig. 10-5C).

If a construction is to be made in box form, it is better to make the lid and box in one piece and saw them apart rather than to try to get two separate constructions to match.

Fig. 10-5. The parts or a machine dovetails are cut together (A). Where corners are not square, the dovetail angled are kept in line (B). The bottom of a drawer can be hidden in the bottom dovetail (C).

Where one part of a joint has to fit into another so its ends are buried, it must be cut to exact length. Where a part goes through, there can be a little waste for planing later, but this cannot be much on the part with dovetails, or it will interfere with removing the waste wood.

It is often possible to mark out and saw several dovetailed ends, such as a batch of drawer sides, while they are held together in a vise. Except for the front piece, which has to be detailed, marking is then restricted to depth lines on each piece and lines squared across the adjoining ends.

Dado And Other Joints

When a piece like a shelf has to be supported by an upright, it is usually recessed into a groove, and this is the basic *dado* or *housing* joint.

TYPES OF DADO JOINTS

How much is cut out for the dado depends on the thickness of the wood. Too much must not be taken out, or the wood will be weakened; but the groove must be deep enough to support the other piece (Fig. 11-1).

The dado can be cut in much the same way as described for making lap joints, but the cuts are longer. If there is doubt about being able to control the saw on a wide board, a piece of straight wood can be clamped on as a guide. With a suitable traveling guide, it may be possible to make the cut with a table saw. It would be easier to make the cut accurate with a radial arm saw. A wobble saw or a dado head is more appropriate to cuts with the grain, but leaves a ragged edge when used.

This is the joint where the old-woman's-tooth type of hand router is used to level the bottom of the groove after most of the waste has been removed with a chisel. A power router can be used to remove the waste and will leave a smooth bottom.

Fig. 11-1. This type of dado joint is visible from both sides of the upright.

Stopped Dado

In bookcase construction it is better if the front of the groove does not show. so a stopped dado is used (Fig. 11-2). The piece at the front that is not cut is kept to a minimum; ¼ in. is about right. Make sure the forward part of the cut on the shelf is neat by using a knife to mark the edge deeply, and bevel against this with a chisel before sawing.

If the stopped dado is to be cut completely by hand. chop out to the full width and depth near the closed end. but leave a little spare in the length of the groove (Fig. 11-2B). How much is cut in this way depends on the craftsman. but about an inch will do. This is to allow movement of the saw in a pared groove against the cut line (Fig. 11-2C). The saw will probably hit the end of the slot. but this will not matter if there is a little waste left there to be removed as a final step. Waste is removed with a chisel and router.

Fig. 11-2. The stopped dado joint (A) is ideally suited, for appearances, to bookcase construction. Paring out about an inch of the groove at the closed end of the groove (B) makes room for saw movement later (C).

104

Dadoes for Extra Strength

The ordinary dado joint brings side grain against end grain, which is not very satisfactory for gluing. This does not matter in many constructions, where other parts of the assembly relieve the dado joints of much strain; but where extra strength seems desirable, there are ways of strengthening. A fillet of wood can be glued in the angle underneath (Fig. 11-3A), or screws can be driven inconspicuously from below (Fig. 11-3B).

The joint can be strengthened by giving it a dovetail form on one or both edges (Fig. 11-3C). This entails sawing the sides of the dado carefully, with the saw at the correct angle. As with other dovetails, a taper ratio of 1:8 is about right. The shelf cut should be deeply scored-in with a knife, and the bevel should be started with a chisel. In smaller work there may be no need for sawing. It is usually sufficient to dovetail only one edge.

Fig. 11-3.Two methods of giving added support to the crossmember of a dado are the use of a fillet (A) and screws (B). Extra strength can be given to the joint by making it take a dovetail form (C).

There can be a further step that gives utmost closeness of joint and the greatest resistance to pulling the shelf from the groove. This is to have a dovetail joint, with another taper in the width of the shelf. Much taper is difficult to give in thin shelves, but the tapered dovetail dado has considerable strength in thicker wood. whether stopped at the front or taken right through (Fig. 11-4). Assembly is by driving the shelf in from the back. One advantage of this joint is that it locks both pieces to shape. so there is a good resistance to warping.

Fig. 11-4. In a tapered dovetail dado the parts are wedged together.

MITERS

A miter joint is usually throught of as being at 45° in a 90° corner (Fig. 11-5A). but it could be at other angles. and even in a 90° corner. two parts of different width necessitate a different angle of cut (Fig. 11-5B). Unusual joints should be laid out carefully. full size. to get the angles. With a 45° miter, a square may be drawn and its diagonal used to give the setting for an adjustable bevel if a miter square or suitable combination square is unavailable. The simplest miter is a plain cut. as in the corner of a picture frame (Fig. 11-5C).

Fig. 11-5. Where parts meet, the neatest joint on the surface is a miter, which is 45° if the parts are the same width (A), but another angle (B) if they are different. The simplest miter is a plain cut (C).

Tools and Techniques for Mitering

Although the ends might be cut to fit exactly with no more than the usual bench tools, there are devices that facilitate fast, accurate cutting. A miter box (Fig. 11-6A) provides a guide for a backsaw. A more elaborate metal guide uses the same principle with more precision. Planing can be done on a special shuting board (Fig. 11-6B).

In a light picture frame it is usual to use glue and drive nails both ways (Fig. 11-6C). There are corner clamps for holding the molding during nailing. The simplest has screws that merely provide a grip. This arrangement is satisfactory, providing the joint is located closely. Another type has a screw which not only holds the parts but pushes them tightly

Fig. 11-6. Ways of ensuring accurate cutting and shaping.

together. usually with a roller arrangement against the rabbets.

A table saw with a fine-tooth blade will cut miters accurately if it has a suitable sliding guide (Fig. 11-6D). For many purposes there will be no need to plane or cut the meeting surfaces after this sawing. Another power tool that will true miters is a sanding disk, providing it is equipped with a table at right angles to its surface and a sliding guide that can be set to the angle required (Fig. 11-6E).

When the joint is larger or under more strain than can be resisted by glue and nails, there are other ways of constructing it. There may be dowels arranged in the same way as nails, or diagonally across the joint and taken right through if the exposed ends will not spoil the appearance (Fig. 11-7A).

There may be stub dowels at right angles to the surfaces, but clamping this sort of joint brings a problem. One way of getting sufficient pressure is to glue or screw triangular blocks on to take a clamp (Fig. 11-7B). They are removed after the glue has set.

Pieces of veneer can be glued into saw cuts (Fig. 11-7C) or thicker pieces may form keys in grooves made in the meeting surfaces (Fig. 11-7D). In a load-bearing structure which would

Fig. 11-7. Strengthening pieces can be fitted across the joints (A through D), or the miter can be combined with another joint (E).

look better with a miter on the face, there can be a bridle joint with one face mitered (Fig. 11-7E).

EXPANSION JOINTS

As wood takes up and loses moisture, it expands and contracts, mostly in the width. Most furniture is not exposed to greatly varying changes in heat or humidity, so properly seasoned wood may be expected to remain fairly stable. However, very wide boards may expand or contract enough to affect joints or cause splitting if precautions are not taken. With modern plywood and other materials to use for wide surfaces, the problem is no longer acute, as these manufactured boards should maintain their size.

If solid wood is used for a panel, it should not be glued into the grooved frame but should be free to move. A thicker panel may have its edge thinned, and this could be used as a decorative feature (Fig. 11-8A).

A solid wooden tabletop must be attached in a way that allows for movement. This can be done with buttons fixed to the top and having tongues to engage with grooves in the framework below (Fig. 11-8B) without glue. A groove may be

Fig. 11-8. Expansion and contraction must be allowed for (A and B) with natural wood, but with manufactured board there may be direct screwing (C).

plowed the full length to take serveral buttons, or notches may be cut for each button. If the top is made from a manufactured board, it can be fixed in the same way, although, since it remains a stable size, pocket screws could be used (Fig. 11-8C).

At one time, tongue-and-groove boards were used extensively in all kinds of construction as a means of covering large areas without gaps. Manufactured boards have taken over for most of these applications. but in furniture there are sometimes occasions when tongue-and-groove boards are still applicable. A tongue fitting into a groove (Fig. 11-9A) may be used to provide a better glue area than a simple butt joint. While this is good construction the main use of tongue-and-groove joints is in taking care of expansion and contraction. The area of the back of the cabinet, for instance, is covered by several boards about 6 in. wide. Their ends are nailed or screwed. but the joints between them are dry. To improve the appearance on the front there may be chamfers, and there could be a bend on one (Fig. 11-9B) so that widening or narrowing of the gap is not so obvious.

glued   front

Fig. 11-9. Before the days of wide panels of plywood and other manufactured board, narrow pieces had to be joined to make up a width. This may still be done for decorative effect, using a simple tongue and groove (A) or a joint with a bead on the front (B).

At one time there were special matched planes for making tongue-and-groove boards. but these are no longer available. The special plane cut both sides of the tongue at the same time, but the tongue can be made by working two rabbets with a hand plane. table saw. or router.

LIPPING

Good quality cabinet wood has always been expensive, and for less noticeable parts something of lesser quality may be used. Besides economy there are places where plywood or blockboard would actually be more appropriate than solid wood. In many places the substitute material has to be given an edge of the same wood as the main structure for the sake of appearance. however. This is lipping.

With solid wood it may be satisfactory to merely glue the lip on (Fig. 11-10A). With plywood or other manufactured board that presents end grain to the joint, this may not be sufficiently secure. Using fine nails, which are punched below the surface and stopped, is not really a craftsmanlike way of giving extra security. It is better to use a tongue-and-groove joint (Fig. 11-10B). To secure an exact match, the lip may be made slightly wide and worked to size after the glue has set.

For a shelf or the bottom of a cabinet, a piece of comparatively thin plywood may be as strong as a piece of thicker solid wood that it replaces, but its edge has to be disguised. It can be glued and pinned in a rabbeted front piece (Fig. 11-10C). If the plywood is thick enough, the joint will be improved if there is a tongue on the plywood mating with a groove in the lip (Fig. 11-10D). The ends of a shelf may have solid wood below the plywood to fit into a dado joint (Fig. 11-10E), and the rear edge may have a stiffening strip or may be supported on a ledge across the back of the cabinet.

There are occasions when, for the sake of appearance on both sides, thin plywood panels fit into a front piece lipped both ways (Fig. 11-10F). There will have to be some crosspieces between the panels as well, and a lengthwise strip at the back edge if this is exposed. In many constructions this can be avoided by using blockboard or similar material of suitable thickness.

If the builtup assembly is plywood over a frame and the plywood is unsupported for most of its area, there is a risk of it distorting. The usual distortion is a concavity. The prevention is to face the other side as well. In a builtup door, for example, the inside should be faced with something of comparable type, although it need not have the high-quality surface of the front panel. In such a door the simplest construction is to take the plywood to the edges of the main framing and use a lip all around that matches the plywood (Fig. 11-1G).

HINGES

Correct hinging calls for care rather than a high degree of skill. If the hinge mounts on the surface, there is little trouble

Fig. 11-10. Techniques for lipping or applying a stiff, attractive edge to plywood or other manufactured board.

except to see that the door has enough clearance along its edge that it does not make contact and bind before it has shut fully.

Some hinges are decorative, but for many pieces of furniture, the hinge has to come in the joint. The basic hinge of this type is a *butt hinge*. If such a hinge is examined, it will be seen that when the two flaps are closed to a parallel position there is a gap between them (Fig. 11-11A). This is to allow for a door or lid closing without the adjoining surfaces touching and stopping it.

In the best construction the two flaps are recessed into both surfaces (Fig. 11-11B). The knuckle has to stand clear of the surfaces, or the door will not swing far without binding on the door frame. How much clearance depends on the item being made. If the door will have to swing right back, the whole circle of the knuckle should be clear (Fig. 11-11C).

If the hinge is recessed entirely into the door, it will swing away with more clearance from the post. The center of the hinge knuckle should be level with the surface of the door or slightly away from it, even if the door does not have to swing right back. Recessing the hinge completely into the door so the

Fig. 11-11. Hinges have to be fitted so there is no ugly gap between the meeting surfaces while allowing the door or lid to swing clear.

other flap is only on the surface of the post is not good cabinetmaking practice, as all the weight of the door is taken by the screws in the post. It is all right to put the knuckle on the surface, but make a sloping cut into the post for the flap (Fig. 11-11D).

One of the few occasions when the knuckle of the hinge may come within the thickness of the wood is in a box lid which is to be stopped at a never vertical position. The meeting edges are beveled and the hinges recessed far enough for the edges to meet and act as stops (Fig. 11-11E).

When you are marking for hinges, take care to see that the knuckles will all be in line, otherwise there will be distortion or strain, and movement of the screws. The length of a recess is best marked from the hinge itself. A gauge is set to the amount the flap is to be recessed in both directions (Fig. 11-12A). Marks across the grain should be cut in with a knife. For small hinges it may be possible to cut deep enough across the ends with a chisel. Otherwise use a fine saw diagonally, not only at the ends but at a few intermediate points to break up the waste. Use a chisel to follow the saw at the ends (Fig. 11-12B).

It is unwise to chop much with a chisel along the gauge lines, but there may be some light cuts on the waste side, then the first of the waste is pared out (Fig. 11-12C). In these shallow recesses it is very easy to go too deep. Try the hinge as cutting progresses. If a cut goes too far it may be possible to back out the hinge with veneer or paper.

Fig. 11-12. Cutting the recess for a hinge is done by shallow saw cuts followed by chisel cuts.

There will have to be a trial assembly, and maybe more than one, before the door or lid moves satisfactorily. It is usually possible to put all the screws through the flap into the door, but then only use one screw in the other flap of each hinge for a trial movement. If all is well, the other screws may be driven. Otherwise. a single screw is withdrawn and driven through another hole to give a corrected position, until the action is satisfactory. A sliver of wood can then be used to plug any wrong hole before all screws are finally driven.

Hinges come with holes drilled and countersunk to take screws of a particular size. As it is important that screw heads should not foul each other and prevent the hinge closing, it is necessary to have screws of the right size and drive them squarely so they go flush into the countersinks. If screws of another size have to be used. prepare the holes in the hinges before doing other work.

Wood For Furniture

Although many man-made and other materials are now used in furniture, wood is still the first choice, particularly for structural parts. There is an attractiveness about wood that is lacking in most other materials. Apart from its appearance, it can be worked without great skill and without the need for elaborate equipment. Manufactured and natural forms of wood make up the bulk of materials used in making built-in furniture.

CHARACTERISTICS OF LUMBER

Wood varies in appearance, quality, characteristics, and flaws. These variations provide much of its attraction. They can be made use of to provide interest and beauty.

As wood comes from trees, possible sizes depend on the original tree. Some trees grow tall and slender and so produce long, narrow boards. Others tend to have thick trunks of no great height, so that boards may be of considerable widths but no great length. Most furniture-making woods are available in all sizes likely to be needed, but it sometimes happens that a particular choice of wood may result in suitable sizes being unavailable.

In any tree a part of the wood is *heartwood*, and around it there is *sapwood* (Fig. 12-1A). As the tree grows, more layers

117

are formed on the outside, and some of the inner sapwood changes into heartwood. The annual rings form the grain marking. In some woods there is a pronounced difference in appearance between sapwood and heartwood. In other woods it is difficult to distinguish them. In general, heartwood is much more durable than sapwood, but there are some woods in which there is little difference durability. Where possible, all wood used for furniture should be heartwood.

As a tree grows, *shakes* may develop. These are cracks that may go around the grain as cup or ring shakes (Fig. 12-1B) or across the grain as heart or star shakes (Fig. 12-1C). These do not affect the quality of the wood, but furniture wood has to be cut around them. When a tree has been felled, it has to be seasoned to dry out the sap to a controlled small amount. Cracks may develop during drying, particularly at the ends. These do not affect quality or other characteristics, but they will have to be allowed for and cut around when preparing furniture parts.

Fig. 12-1. The middle of a tree produces heartwood (A) the most durable wood, but there may be flaws: cup or ring shakes (B) and heart or star shakes (C).

Wood will always absorb and give up moisture with changes in humidity. This affects the stability of the wood. There is little effect along the grain, but a board may expand in its width as it takes up moisture and shrink as it loses moisture. It will also warp, and the risk of warping and its probable direction is related to the way the board is cut from the tree.

CONVERSION OF LOGS TO LUMBER

If boards are cut straight across the log, a board with the grain marks across the thickness is unlikely to warp at all (Fig. 12-2A); but boards nearer the circumference will tend to become hollow (Fig. 12-2B). If the end of a board is examined, the board's relation to the whole section of tree can be visualized and the risk of warping estimated. A convenient way to remember what may happen is to consider the curved grain rings as trying to straighten out (Fig. 12-2C). If the wood is in a round or square section. distortion is likely to be a shrinking in the direction of the grain (Fig. 12-2D) as the wood dries.

Fig. 12-2. Freshly cut boards warp and shrink as they dry, but this is less obvious if the grain lines are across the thickness.

119

Sometimes wood is cut to give the best grain appearance. To get the maximum number of boards with attractive markings, they are cut from the outside inwards (Fig. 12-3A). Besides grain there are *medullary rays*, which radiate from the center outwards. In many woods they are invisible, but in some woods they are sufficiently prominent to provide a decorative effect if the wood is cut along their lines. This is particularly so in some types of oak. A radially cut board is then described as *quarter sawn, figured oak, wainscot oak,* or *silver grain* (Fig. 12-3B). Cutting many boards exactly radially results in much waste so it is more usual to make the cuts in layers (Fig. 12-3C) so that all but the outermost boards may be expected to show markings from the medullary rays. Wood cut this way will be more expensive, but in suitable types the effect is very attractive.

Fig. 12-3. Wood may be cut to get the best appearance of grain (A), or to use the figuring of rays in oak and some other woods (B and C).

LUMBER SIZES AND GRADES

Much furniture-grade wood is sold in nonstandard sizes or prepared to suit the customer. The owner of a shop with suitable equipment will find it most economical to buy wood in stock sections and cut it down to suit his needs Even then, if stock sections from the local yard can be used, there will be a saving in cost and effort. Standard sizes are most applicable to lumber used for house construction and similar work, but may be found with the higher quality woods needed for furniture.

Grades

Lumber may be offered in two grades: *select* and *common*. Select may be subdivided into A, B, C, and D in decreasing quality. Common lumber starts where select leaves off and is graded into 1, 2, 3, and 4 in descending quality. The main difference between select and common lumber is in the ability to take a finish where the grain shows through. Grades A and B obviously are just about free of blemishes or defects in the grain, but these may be more obvious in grades C and D. Common grades are suitable for use where they do not have to take a finish or where appearance is unimportant. Grades 1 and 2 have uses in internal work in furniture, but grades 3 and 4 may have too many defects—such as large knots, knotholes, or confused, rough grain—to be used in furniture.

It is possible that a board with a low grade because of a defect in one place may yield wood of adequate quality in another part. For economy the buyer may not want to buy wood of a higher grade than necessary. If you have an opportunity to look over the stock in a lumberyard, it is often possible to find economical pieces you can use by cutting around defects yourself.

Sizes

Lumber is sized as it is sawn. Machine planing takes off at least $1/8$ in. This means that a piece of lumber described as 2 by 4 in. which has been machine planed all round will actually be about $1\frac{3}{4}$ by $3\frac{3}{4}$ in. The term *board* is applied to wood for sale that is over 8 in. wide and less than 2 in. thick. Smaller pieces may be called *strips*. Larger sections may be called *timbers* although in some places *timber* is a word used as an alternative to *lumber*.

Lumberyards that may not cut the wood to size on the premises may keep stock lengths in multiples of 2 ft, from 6 ft upward. Purchases should be arranged to allow for this. Charges may be according to length and section, but it is advisable to know what is meant by *board foot* in case that is the method of quoting prices. This reduces the size to the equivalent of a square foot 1 in. thick. Hence a piece of wood

1 ft square and 1 in thick is one board foot. So is a piece 2 in. wide and 6 ft long by 1 in. thick. A thicker piece has to be reduced to 1 in. by increasing the surface area, so a piece of wood 2 in. thick need only be half a square foot on the surface to represent one board foot.

There is an advantage in buying in quantity rather than just getting wood for the project at hand. There are certain stock sections that find a use in many pieces of built-in furniture, and it is economical to build up a store so you can take wood from the shelf or rack as needed. It would be false economy to buy unusual material that might never be needed again, but even then, much of the joy of amateur craftsmanship is in designing furniture around available material.

Because of difficulty in obtaining long or wide pieces in some woods (caused by the sizes of trees), extra wide or long pieces may cost proportionately more than smaller pieces. It is always advisable to visit a lumberyard armed with your detailed cutting list; then wood from stock may be found to suit items economically. This is much better than totaling all the pieces of a certain section and asking for one long piece, which may carry a premium because of its length.

Similar arguments apply to widths. It is usually most economical to accept the narrowest pieces that will suit your purpose rather than to ask for wider boards to cut down. However, there are exceptions. Very narrow pieces may be cut from the waste from cutting large boards and may be sapwood. Narrow strips may be cut from branches. A wide board has to be cut from the trunk of the tree and should be all heartwood. The best wood is more likely to be in the wide piece, and if this is particularly wanted, it may be advisable to buy a wide board and cut it down, even if it costs more than the equivalent narrow pieces.

WOOD TYPES

Wood is very broadly divided into hardwoods and softwoods. Although most hardwoods are harder than most softwoods, the names are not really very apt. Hardwoods are those trees that have broad leaves, nearly all of which are lost during the winter. Softwoods are trees with needle leaves, which are mostly retained during the winter. It is the pines, firs, spruces, and similar trees that make up the softwoods that the average woodworker will handle. All the better woods that are used for furniture, particularly where a polished finish is used, are hardwoods.

It is difficult to keep track of all the kinds of wood. Although certain woods are accepted for particular purposes and are in fairly regular supply, there are many others that are equally suitable for the same purposes. There are supposed to be upwards of 3000 separate species of trees with commercial value, so any advice on woods can only be regarded as a guide.

Quite often a piece of built-in furniture will have to match some existing furniture, and that will settle what wood is to be used, at least for the visible parts. Sometimes, however, contrasting wood can be quite effective. A room with dark furniture may benefit from building in something with light facing, or vice versa.

The use of the furniture should be considered. Something in a child's room may get rougher treatment than a similar thing elsewhere, so the wood should be one that will take knocks without showing them much and should certainly not be likely to splinter. A corner cupboard may not be at much risk from knocks because of its position, so a softer wood could be sufficiently durable.

Some of the more choice woods are very expensive. They may still be worth having, but it is sometimes possible to use a cheaper wood with a sufficiently similar grain marking, then finish it with stain and polish to produce an effective piece of furniture at a much lower price. Of course, if the final finish is to be paint, it is more important to have wood that will finish smoothly, with no pronounced grain.

Softwoods

Although softwoods grow in many parts of the world, those used by woodworkers are mostly from the northern temperate zones of America, Europe, and Asia. Unfortunately, common names are not always the same, and the same wood may have a different name if it comes from a different place. Some are listed below with their alternate names.

Cedar, Western Red. Soft, reddish-brown, straight grained, and available in long lengths.

Cypress. Grows in swamps. Has a greasy feel and a sour smell. Straight-grained, light brown. Will withstand heat and moisture. Does not take glue very well.

Columbian Pine, Douglas Pine, Oregon Pine, Douglas Fir. One of the harder softwoods, straight-grained, reddish-brown. Raised grain and resin make the wood unsuitable for face work, but it may be used structurally in furniture.

Hemlock. Does not take a fine finish and is more of an external wood than one for furniture.

Larch. Medium texture, easily worked, light orange-brown color.

Pine, Parana. Brazilian wood, pale straw color, and available in wide boards.

Pine, Pitch. Heavy because of considerable resin. Has pronounced grain. Difficult to bring to a good finish.

Other Pines. Eastern white pine and ponderosa pine are light, with little strength. Sugar pine grows into large trees; it will finish smoothly despite large knots, which may be used as a decorative feature. Western white pine is similar. None of these is very durable if exposed.

Redwood, Yellow Deal, Red Deal, Red Pine, Scots Pine, Northern Pine. Reddish-brown, straight-grained, some resin. Suitable for internal construction.

Sequoia, California Redwood. Very large trees, so great lengths and widths obtainable. Rather open and porous, reddish-brown, and straight grained. Not very strong.

Spruce, Sitka, Silver Spruce. A combination of lightness with a strong, straight grain makes this a choice for aircraft construction and yacht spars. Not a furniture choice unless easily obtained.

Spruce, Whitewood, White Deal. Sometimes considered a poorer quality redwood. Near white, with some knots and resin pockets.

Hardwoods

Although a great variety of hardwoods are native to North America, many others are imported because of their special qualities. Distribution varies according to geography and climate. When making traditional furniture, the indigenous wood of the region is often chosen. Some of the woods indigenous to various regions are listed below, but these lists are not exhaustive, and some trees spread over into other regions.

Northern Region. Ash, aspen, basswood, yellow birch, butternut, cherry, elm, hickory, locust, hard maple, oak, walnut.

Central Region. White ash, basswood, beech, buckeye, chestnut, cottonwood, American elm, hackberry, shagbark hickory, locust, hard maple, white oak, sycamore, yellow poplar, walnut.

Appalachian Region. Ash, beech, red oak, white oak, hard maple.

Southern Region. Ash, basswood, beech, birch, cottonwood, elm, hackberry, hickory, locust, maple, red and cherry-bark oak, pecan, sweet and red gum, sycamore, black willow.

There are some very hard woods, such as greenheart, which will sink in water; but these do not have furniture uses. The softest and lightest of what are technically hardwoods is balsa—which is softer and lighter than most softwoods. It has no normal furniture application.

The woods listed below are hardwood examples, which may provide comparisons when other woods are being considered.

Ash. Straight, rather coarse grain. Valued for its springiness and bending qualities.

Basswood, Lime. Light, close-grained; easy to work and suitable for carving.

Beech, Red or White. Tough, close grain. Used for tools. Very good for turning on lathe.

Chestnut. Looks and works like oak, but has no figuring when quarter-sawn.

125

Elm. Durable, with confused grain that resists splitting. Not of much use in furniture except traditional designs.

Gaboon. Nondurable African wood that looks like mahogany. Used for lightweight plywood.

Red gum, Sweet Gum, Satin Walnut. Soft, even brown color with little sign of grain. Stains well. Twists and warps if not built into other parts.

Maple. Varies from light yellow to brown.

Mahogany, Spanish and Cuban. Rich brown with close grain. Original furniture mahogany, but there are many more.

Mahogany, Honduras; Baywoods. Lightweight with light brown color. A furniture wood.

Mahogany, African. There are several of these, and not all true mahoganies; but some are suitable for furniture.

Red Oak. The usual open-grained brown oak, with a pink shade present. Has figuring in quarter-sawn boards. Large boards obtainable.

Oak, Engligh. The oak used for medieval ships and furniture. Brown, open-grained, with prominent figuring when quarter-sawn. Very strong and durable.

Oak, Japunese and Austrian. More mellow and easier to work than English oak. Good furniture woods.

Poplar, yellow; Canary Wood; American Whitewood.. Even, close-grained, yellow wood, Varying quality, but usually easy to work. Similar to basswood and sometimes confused with it.

Sapele. Looks like mahogany. Its attractive grain may be difficult to work. Used for making plywood.

Sycamore. Whitish-yellow. close-grained wood with sometimes a figure or ripple marking visible in the grain. Good for turning on lathe. Its near white color makes it suitable for use with food.

Teak. This is a dark brown wood that bleaches to near white in the sun. It may be difficult to work because of its resin. It is very durable even when not treated in any way. Not usual for furniture.

Walnut, American Black Walnut. A shade of purple mixed with dark brown. Takes a good finish.

Manufactured Wood

All wood is prepared for use by being cut from logs and seasoned. This may be considered a manufacturing process, but there are a number of wood forms, particularly in panels, in which manufacturing is taken further. These have revolutionized furniture making and made the construction of broad surfaces and panels much easier, and with results superior to anything achieved with solid wood. The use of plywood or other manufactured wood panels is good, modern cabinetmaking practice. The only places where these things would not be appropriate would be in reproduction work or the repair of antiques.

PLYWOOD

In its early days plywood was often rough and insecurely bonded by the less satisfactory glues then available. Modern plywood is extremely strong and stable, and finishes to match anything on solid wood are possible.

Plywood Veneers

Plywood is made from *veneers*, which are thin slices of wood. Most veneers for plywood are rotary-cut, with a knife slicing off the correct thickness in a long length from a rotating log (Fig. 13-1A). The grain marking will not be the same as that from wood cut across by sawing. As the log rotates, similar grain markings will be repeated at each complete turn. If a plywood panel is examined, this can be seen as a repeat of the grain pattern across the panel. The distance between these repeats is the same as the circumference at the time of the cut.

With veneers cut this way the grain marking will not be a match with any solid wood from the same species of tree. This does not usually matter, as the color should match and the grain appearance can be quite attractive.

Veneers of some wood are sliced with a knife across the wood as in Fig. 13-1B, or they may be cut with a saw as in Fig. 13-1C. In both cases the width is limited by the thickness of the original piece of wood. Such veneers are not usually made into plywood, but they may be used to face it. They have the same grain markings as solid wood from the same tree.

Fig. 13-1. Veneers may be cut continously around a log (A) by slicing (B) or sawing (C).

The thickness of veneers made into plywood varies. Some aircraft plywood has three layers within a total thickness of 1/25 in., or 1 mm. In furniture plywood a veneer thickness about 1½ mm is common, but veneer thickness has to be regulated according to the total thickness required. Much early plywood had three veneers, hence the name 3-ply. Many other numbers of veneers are used, but 3-ply is common for thinner sheets. The three plies may be the same thickness

(Fig. 13-2A), or the center one may be thicker (Fig. 13-2B) to give a more balanced strength. Whatever the number of veneers, the outer ones are normally in the same direction (Fig. 13-2C).

Glue in plywood is normally a synthetic type, usually with a good resistance to dampness, so the plywood remains flat and does not expand and contract to any extent that will matter.

Fig. 13-2. Plywood may have three plies of equal thickness (A), or the center ply may be thicker (B). Outer grains are usually aligned (C). A compensating veneer opposite the face side (D) reduces warpage.

Many woods are used for making plywood, but there are some which are unsuitable for rotary cutting of veneers or are not obtainable in suitable sizes. Some woods only show the beauty of their grain if crosscut; rotary cutting, even if the wood permitted this, would not result in as attractive an appearance. Some woods are rare and expensive, so their use in solid form would be wasteful. Many of these may be cut into veneers so that their beauty can be spread as far as possible, the veneers being put on a cheaper base material.

Plywood is ideal for this, and panels may be bought already faced with veneers of rare woods, either as an overall arrangement of strips butted together side by side, or with veneer pieces arranged in a pattern. Normally the face veneers are thinner than those that go to make up the plywood, and it is usual to put a compensating veneer (not necessarily of choice wood) on the opposite side (Fig. 13-2D). This balances stresses in the plywood and resists any tendency to warping.

Sizes and Grades

Plywood is made in panels of many sizes. A common width is 4 ft. and most panels are 8 ft long; but longer panels are made. Thicknesses start at $^3/_{16}$ in. or less and go up to about ¾ in. Some manufacturers use metric thicknesses, from 4 to 18 mm. The number of plies in a thickness varies. A larger number should result in a stiffer panel for the same thickness: 5 ply wood ¼ in. thick should be stiffer than 3-ply wood ¼ in. thick.

Most plywood manufacturers divide their products into interior and exterior grades, with the latter able to withstand outdoor weather. A marine grade is superior to the exterior grade and suitable for use in boats. Within each grade there may be many variations of veneer. A cabinet-quality veneer is without flaws; this may be on one or both outer surfaces, depending on the intended use. A less important surface may have flaws such as knots (or knots may have been cut out and plugged), and there may be small splits in the veneers.

The grade of veneer in the core may vary. For greatest strength and for some exterior applications, it is important to have good-quality veneers inside. Elsewhere inferior veneers may be used inside without affecting the use of the plywood. Edge joints between internal veneers should meet for greatest strength, but for some purposes slight gaps will not matter. Where plywood of these lesser qualities can be used, the price should be less.

BLOCK BOARD AND CHIPBOARDS

Thick plywood is expensive, and alternatives are used, most often with a core made of solid wood strips, collectively called *blockboard*. There are outer veneers as in plywood, but the center is made up of solid strips, with the pieces glued to each other and to the veneers. The grain of the inner pieces crosses that of the veneers, which are often thicker than the outer plies of plywood. Blockboard with narrow strips inside may be called *laminboard* (Fig. 13-3A). If wider pieces are used, it is *battenboard* (Fig. 13-3B). In some forms the outer veneers are a double thickness, which gives an increased resistance to any tendency to twist or warp.

Fig. 13-3. There are alternatives to the thicker plywood, with solid wood cores (A and B) or wood particles mixed with synthetic resin (C and D).

A thicker board made up from wood particles embedded in synthetic resin may be described as *particle board* or *chipboard* (Fig. 13-3C). This is unattractive and so has to be covered when used in exposed places.

Chipboard may be veneered during manufacture, either with wood veneer or plastic with a wood grain appearance. These boards, in many stock sizes, may be veneered on edges and ends as well as the surfaces (Fig. 13-3D) and sold under various trade names. If a design can be arranged to take a stock size of board, this material will make attractive worktops, shelves, and room dividers. If a veneered board has to be cut and the cut edge will be exposed, it has to be veneered by hand. Matching veneers are available from some makers. These may be self-adhesive, or they may have to be fixed with a contact adhesive. As the base material is a plastic resin rather than wood, many ordinary wood glues do not suit it.

There are problems in using screws or other fasteners with chipboard, but there are special attachments, and plugs can be glued in to take screws.

HARDBOARD

Wood pulp may be manufactured into boards. There are many grades, mainly dependent on the density of the boards. Loosely bonded boards are used for insulation, and there are others more like card than wood; but quite a hard material can be made when a suitable bonding agent is used and there is sufficient compression. For furniture construction this hardboard has some uses for cheap backs of cabinets or drawer bottoms. *Masonite* is one well known make.

Hardboard is commonly available in sheet sizes similar to those of plywood; ⅛ in. is the usual thickness, although others are made. In the basic sheet there is one hard, smooth surface, and the other is rough and patterned. It is possible to get sheets smooth on both sides, and there are panels given .fluted and other patterned effects.

Providing the original surface is not broken through by tools or sanding, it can be extremely hard wearing in the better grades. The softer and cheaper qualities are not really suitable for permanent furniture.

Some of the better boards are given a treatment by oil or some other means during manufacture that gives them a tougher, water-resistant quality. They may be described as *oil tempered*. Although these are intended mainly for exposed surfaces, they are the best choice for furniture. Hardboard takes most of the finishes used on ordinary wood, and the smooth surface without blemishes makes a good base for paint.

PREPARED STRIPS

Besides wood in rectangular sections there are many other stock sections obtainable, and some of these can be used in built-in furniture. A visit to a lumberyard or a supplier specializing in woodwork supplies will show what is available.

There are, for example, round sections. In the smaller sizes these are described as dowel rods, and they are in suitable hardwoods for use in making dowel joints; but as the lengths are often 3 ft or more, it is possible to use them as rails or posts in some constructions. Larger sections may be intended as broom handles, but they have uses for such things as a rail to take clothes hangers.

There are many standard molding sections. Some of these are designed to cover plywood edges or give a finish to corner-lapped joints. In some constructions the use of moldings allows simpler joints between parts, as they can be covered. Anyone proud of his woodworking skill will want to make his furniture by acceptable methods, but restrained use of manufactured moldings will often enhance the result.

The larger moldings are made of white pine or other softwood, so they require a painted finish. But there are hardwood moldings usable for cabinetwork; picture frame moldings are examples.

Decorative pieces of wood may be bought to glue onto furniture. These may be embossed to look like carving. The fastidious cabinetmaker is likely to feel that they are inferior substitutes for the real thing and avoid them.

Working With Metals And Plastics

Although wood is used more than any other material in furniture, there are other materials which are used to supplement it or replace it for some purposes. These include metals and plastics.

Most amateur craftsmen find woodworking easier than the equivalent work on other materials. However, anyone who wants to have a thorough mastery of furniture making should be able to work in other materials.

ALUMINUM

The most useful metal for many parts of built-in furniture is aluminum. Pure aluminum is a soft metal. Most of the metal available in sheets, rods, and tubes is actually an alloy, with comparatively small quantities of other metals added mainly to give hardness. The attraction of aluminum is its good resistance to corrosion without the need for plating or other surface treatment.

STEEL

Mild steel, sometimes described loosely as iron, is commonly used in cabinets. Mild steel is iron with a very small amount of carbon added. It cannot be hardened and tempered in the way tool steel can.

Iron and steel will rust, and there does not have to be much moisture present. Unprotected steel may have some limited usefulness in places where it does not show, but for exposed parts of furniture, something has to be done to protect it. Ready-made steel fittings are usually plated in some way. The amateur worker is unlikely to have plating facilities available for anything he makes from steel, but in some cases it may be worthwhile having plating done professionally.

The alternative is to paint the metal. There should be no sign of rust on the metal before painting. The surface may be rubbed with an abrasive immediately before painting. With new steel parts this may be enough preparation, but if there is any doubt, the surface should be coated with a rust-inhibiting fluid before painting. Painting over rust will result in the corrosion continuing, and rust spots will eventually show through.

The word *stainless* in *stainless steel* is a relative term. There is no one stainless steel that is immune to attack by everything. There are stainless steels that are unaffected by the majority of common liquids and gases. Some are made to resist corrosion in particular situations, but they may be quite vulnerable in others. Consequently it is advisable to check that the stainless steel being used in furniture will suit the circumstances.

Most generally available stainless steels are suitable for domestic uses, but if the metal is an exotic one obtained from surplus or some other sources, it may not be suitable. Most stainless steels are hard and difficult to work, so they may not be very attractive to a worker with only hand metalworking tools; but the results achieved can be quite attractice.

COPPER AND ITS ALLOYS

Copper is a reddish metal that is ductile and easily shaped, making it suitable for beating into bowls and similar things, but it does not have much use in furniture making. Copper is mixed with other metals to produce well known alloys.

Brass is an alloy of copper and zinc giving a yellow metal with a good resistance to corrosion. The proportion of the constituents affects the qualities and appearance of the brass, as does the method of production. Rolled brass is ductile, and sheets can be easily bent and formed. Extruded and drawn brass is easier to machine. Drawn brass will usually bend, but some extruded brass produced especially for machining is brittle and will crumble and break if bent.

Copper alloyed tin and certain other metals produce combinations often loosely described as bronzes. These usually have a deeper, more golden tone than brass. Some bronzes have very good resistance to salt, as well as most other corrosives, combined with good strength. Hence they are used at sea, but they are also advisable for furniture in the salt-laden atmosphere of a seaside house.

TOOLS

Metalwork associated with built-in furniture is usually fairly simple—in altering a bought fitting, cutting to length, bending sheet metal to make a bracket, or bringing some part to a finish. It is advisable to do metalwork away from the bench normally used for woodworking. Filings and swarf may become embedded in wood, and the different sort of waste produced when metal is worked may soil wood, either the working surface or the wood parts of a piece of furniture.

A metalworking vise is necessary if much work is to be done in metal; this may be a small one with a built-in clamp so it can be mounted on the edge of a table when needed. An anvil is also needed; this may be a plain iron block of no particular size, with a flat top and enough weight that it won't move about when something is hammered on it. A woodworking hammer may be the only one you need, but a ball peen (Fig. 14-1) is better.

Holes are made with the usual Morse-pattern twist drills. While cheap carbon-steel drills may be good enough for woodwork, it is better to have high-speed drills for metal. They keep their edge longer and are the only type to use for most stainless steel. Holes in metal should always be located with a dot from a center punch. For precision drilling and to avoid breaking drills in thicker metal, it is advisable to mount an electric drill in a bench stand. Countersinking in metal is better done with a simple spade bit turned slowly in a carpenter's brace than with a fast-turning rose bit.

Sheet metal can be cut by hand with snips (center right, Fig. 14-1). One side of the cut tends to be distorted, but this is a convenient means of shaping screwed plates and brackets to be used in furniture. The alternative is a nibbler, which is either a self-contained power tool or an attachment for a drill.

Thicker metal is cut with a hacksaw (top, Fig. 14-1). Blades may be bought with different sizes of teeth. For tubes and thin metal, fine teeth are needed, but for thicker, solid metal, cutting is quicker with coarser teeth. When cutting harder metals, such as stainless steel, it is important to keep a saw or drill cutting. If pressure is relaxed and the tool allowed to rub without actually cutting, the edge is very rapidly worn away.

Fig. 14-1. Some basic metalworking tools. Top: The hacksaw frame is the compact type; others have an extending handle. Left: Side cutters, for cutting wire and nails. Center: Pliers. Besides providing insulation, the plastic handles give a comfortable grip. Right: Snips, or shears, for sheet metal. Bottom: The file has a plastic handle molded on; the hammer has a ball peen for riveting.

The metalworking equivalent of a plane is a file. A good first file is a half-round about 10 in. long with second-cut teeth, but files of other sections and sizes and with other teeth are useful, including some quite small ones for getting into places like keyhole slots and for removing raggedness around the edges of quantity-produced fittings.

Filing may have to be followed by rubbing with an abrasive cloth. Emery is the traditional abrasive, but there are many others. Rubbing with an abrasive will produce a finely-matted surface, which may approach a gloss if a sufficiently fine abrasive is used; but a high gloss is obtained by using suitable buffing compounds on a power-driven polishing head.

Polishing mops are sold in various forms, but a common type has many layers of cloth disks of about 6 in. diameter. This is driven at 3000 rmp or more, which is enough for centrifugal forces to spin the disks to a hard enough form to take the compound on their circumference and produce a gloss on metal held against them.

Most of the metals used on furniture will not need any special treatment and can be shaped as supplied. Those containing copper can be annealed (softened) to make them easier to shape. In particular, copper and brass heated to redness and allowed to cool will become very ductile. Working and hammering will harden them again. Prolonged hammering may actually cause brittleness to the point of cracking, so when much shaping by hammering has to be done, annealing may have to be done more than once.

Bending sheet metal is best done in the vise, preferably between strips of smooth metal so the vise jaws do not mark the surface. Direct hammering may mark the metal. To avoid this a *drift* can be used. This is a flat-ended piece of steel used as a punch. Very thin metal can often be bent by pushing instead of hammering. The piece to be bent projects above the vise jaws and a piece of wood pushing against it makes a clean bend without marks.

PLASTICS

The word *plastics* covers a whole range of materials with a far greater variety and scope than the many species covered by the word *wood*. Plastics range from extremely hard-and-dense materials to extremely light-and-fine fabrics. (Plastic fabrics are treated in Chapter 16).

Laminates

The most used plastic is plastic laminate, which can provide working surfaces much more durable than wood. *Formica* is one well known brand.

Most plastic laminate is in sheets less than $^1/_{16}$ in. thick. Although it is reasonably strong, it is flexible and could be cracked by flexing or damaged by knocks, so take care in handling and transporting it. Putting it between pieces of plywood is the best way to carry or store it.

Cutting can be done with a fine saw used at a fairly flat angle, with the laminate supported fairly close to the cut edge so it cannot vibrate (Fig. 14-2A). Keeping the saw at a low angle means the maximum number of teeth are in contact, and there is less risk of breaking out. Most plastics get more brittle at low temperatures, so it is always safer to work at a comfortable temperature. Excessive heat should be avoided, as this may cause enough softening to make the material cling to the saw and produce a poor edge.

An edge may be filed, but a low-angled block or shoulder plane will produce a good edge if the blade is sharp and finely set. Use it at an angle, with the edge pointing away from the top surface (Fig. 14-2B). Use this technique also if the edge has to be trued after the laminate has been fixed to wood. There are special scraping tools for finishing laminated edges either square to the surface or at an angle. If you sand an edge, be careful not to let the abrasive cut into the top surface. For hand sanding, wrap the abrasive paper around a block of wood.

Laminates have to be fixed to wood with the adhesive recommended by the maker. Usually this is an impact type, which does not allow of movement once the surfaces have met. To ensure the joint together coming right the first time and to avoid air bubbles, use guide blocks at one end and lower the laminate by curving it (Fig. 14-2C).

Plexiglas

Another useful plastic is *Plexiglas*. The transparent form can be used instead of glass in furniture doors. It can also be sprung around moderate curves without special treatment, so

Fig. 14-2. Thin plastic laminate should be supported while cutting and planing (A and B). Use locating pieces when the joint is made with an impact adhesive (C).

bow-fronted doors may be "glazed" in a way that would be impossible with glass in the home shop.

Plexiglas has a very high gloss on the surface but is easily scratched. Consequently, if it comes protected with paper, this should be left on as long as possible during working. It is also convenient for marking with a pencil. Pad the vise jaws and cover the bench top with smooth hardboard and paper. It is not impossible to restore a polished surface, but it is better to avoid damaging it in the first place.

Sawing and Drilling Plexiglas

Plexiglas may be sawn, filed, and planed in the same way as laminate. It is not advisable to use power saws, since the heat caused by the friction of power sawing may melt the edges, which will bond together again behind the saw or leave a very rough edge. Hand sawing leaves a fairly clean edge that does not require as much work to finish it.

When drilling laminate or Plexiglas, do not use a center punch, but make a dent by twisting a triangular-pointed awl into it (Fig. 14-3A). Holes up to about $^3/_{16}$ in. may be drilled with ordinary Morse twist drills, preferably slowly and by hand. As with sawing, fast power drilling may generate enough heat to melt the edges of the hole and leave them ragged. In a bad case, the plastic may cling to the drill and break. For larger holes there are drills intended for plastics. They have steeper angles of flutes, and this reduces any tendency for the drill to catch. An alternative is to grind the leading edge of a standard drill vertical (Fig. 14-3B).

Fig. 14-3. To make holes in sheet plastics, mark with a square-pointed awl (A). Grind off the cutting edge of larger drills. (B).

If a Plexiglas piece is recessed into a frame in the same way as glass, there is no need for special work on the edges; but the material is very suitable, in clear or colored form, for surface items.

Polishing Plexiglas

Filing or planing is followed by sanding, preferably with two or three progressively finer grades of abrasive, each grade completely removing the scratches produced by the previous grade.

There are special polishes for Plexiglas that follow the sanding stage with two grades of liquid or paste polish. These are used, in turn, on cloth. Remove all trace of the first polish before using the second. Similar work can be done by using pumice powder or even a domestic cleaning powder for the first stage, then a polish intended for silver for the final stage. If the final polish is in the form of an impregnated cloth or pad, it must not have been previously used on metal.

Plexiglas edges can be polished on a buffer in the same way as metal, but the buffer must be reserved for plastic, and a compound intended for plastic must be used on it. Keep the Plexiglas moving so no part of the edge gets very warm. Excessive work on one spot will cause burning of the edge, leaving a rough finish that can only be removed by cutting it away and starting again.

Bending Plexiglas

Plexiglas can be bent after heating. It can be sprung to modest curves without heating. and this is preferable where it can be retained in shape by framing. The main problem with softening to bend is that surfaces may be damaged in the process. Some of the material will soften in hot water. Other grades need more heat. such as may be obtained in a cooking oven. It is necessary to make a mold and cover it with a cloth with as smooth a surface as possible. and certainly no flaws or seams. as the slightest imperfection may mark the softened surface. Handle the softened Plexiglas with smooth gloves. Apart from the material being too hot for bare hands, this reduces the risk of marking. The softened Plexiglas should be quite limp and able to be merely draped around the mold without pressure. Leave it to set, which will not take long. Do not try to hasten setting with cold air or water.

Fixings And Fittings

Most built-in furniture has to be fixed to a wall, ceiling, or floor. It may be possible to make an item so tight in a recess that no attachment is required. Or it may be possible to arrange a part to expand and grip a recess that way. However, in most cases there is a need to fix to the walls if not to the floor or ceiling.

What fastenings are used depends on the type of wall. If it is wood of sufficient thickness to take screws, attaching the furniture to the wall is no different from screwing any other wood parts together. If it is a substantial piece of furniture or something that will be heavily loaded, it may be necessary to check that the woodwork of the wall is itself sufficiently attached to take this additional load. Some decorative wood lining may be adequately fixed for its decorative purpose, but it may not be able to take much of a load. If wood is over the studding, screwing through the wood paneling into the studding is desirable.

In any case, let the screws be as long as possible, providing they do not go right through. Because the length of unthreaded neck gets greater as screws get longer, an excessively long screw that goes through may have less grip than one that just spans the thickness (Fig. 15-1). Drill an

Fig. 15-1. When fixing to wood, a screw of the right length has the better grip.

exploratory hole and check the thickness before settling on the size of screw to use.

ATTACHMENTS TO SOLID WALLS

For solid walls of concrete, brick, stone, or cinder block, it is usually necessary to have some sort of plug into which fastenings may be driven. There are masonry nails, made of hardened steel, that can be driven into many of these surfaces. It is probably advisable to treat these as locating rather than load-bearing fixings. If the load comes sideways, a nail will grip well enough (Fig. 15-2A); but if the load puts a strain in the direction of withdrawal, it is better to use a screw or some form of through fastening (Fig. 15-2B).

Fig. 15-2. Loads are better taken across a fastening (A) than in the direction it was driven (B).

If masonry is laid with mortar lines, it may be possible to pick or chop out mortar and drive in a wood plug, with the grain across so as to give a screw a good grip. The plug can be given a better hold if it is cut on the skew so it is twisted as it is driven home (Fig. 15-3). For recessed mortar lines there are

Fig. 15-3. Where screws are needed in a section of masonry, a wood plug can replace chopped out mortar.

Miller's wedge anchors. These lead anchors are put into the recess in the manner of folding wedges, then the fastening is driven between the wedges.

With masonry there may be plaster which obscures joints, and fastenings will have to be made at selected places without reference to the location of masonry joints, so holes are more likely to be into solid material than into joints. It is possible to get masonry drills with special tips for drilling stone and other hard materials. They may be used with an ordinary electric drill, but their effectiveness is increased if they are made to vibrate with a percussion action as well as to turn. There are special electric drills for this purpose, or adapters can be obtained for plain drills.

A hole may also be made with a special tool driven with a hammer. The round, fluted tool (star drill) has a diamond-shaped point. It is turned between hammer blows and will penetrate most masonry materials. A careful worker can achieve as good a hole with this tool as with a power drill, but there is more risk of cracks radiating as the hole is made. When there is a layer of plaster over brick or stone, it is advisable to get through this with an ordinary drill before using a masonry drill or a tool with a hammer. If the hole in the plaster is slightly larger than that in the harder material, there is less risk of plaster breaking away (Fig. 15-4A).

A hold in masonry is obtained by using a plug which expands when a screw is driven. A simple wood plug can be used successfully. This may be roughly rounded so as to make a drive fit in the hole. However, it is better to use a ready-made plug, of which there are several. A fibrous type (Fig. 15-4B) gives a good grip. When using this type or a wooden plug, consider the screw. If this is only going through a metal plate, part of the unthreaded neck has to go into the wall. If this has to pull its way into the plug at surface level, it may refuse to go or may expand the plug enough to cause the surface of the masonry to break out. It is better to drive the plug a short distance below the surface (Fig. 15-4C) with a punch.

There are plastic anchor plugs which serve the same purpose. Most have a shoulder at surface level and are split so they spread as a screw is driven (Fig. 15-4D). A similar plug made of lead works the same way. For these and other plugs it is important to start with a hole that is a little deeper than the screw is expected to penetrate. The screw cannot be expected to cut its own way farther into the masonry.

Fig. 15-4. When drilling through a brick wall faced with plaster, make the hole in the outer layer larger than that beneath (A). The plug, preferably a fibrous type (B), should be driven slightly below the surface (C) with a punch; plastic anchor plugs (D) serve the same purpose.

Most fastening of built-in furniture with masonry walls will be by wood screws, but where a considerable load has to be taken, it may be better to use a plug that takes a machine screw. These are threaded so the screw enters easily, but farther down the hole the design is such that further screwing causes the anchor to expand in the hole. Usually the anchor plug comes with a matching screw, perhaps with a choice of heads. For heavy loads a large washer under the head increases its grip (Fig. 15-5A).

There are similar plugs for screws into chipboard. Most of these fit ½ in. holes and are made of plastic (Fig. 15-5B). When a screw is driven, the plug expands to grip the hole, but not enough to bulge or burst the chipboard.

Fig. 15-5. A large washer under the head (A) increases the grip of a screw in an anchor plug. Special plastic plugs are made for chipboard (B).

ATTACHMENTS TO HOLLOW WALLS

Attachments often have to be made to hollow walls. There are plastic anchors like those for masonry that expand and have gripping ridges around the outside. They can be bought with flanges that will space panels away from the wall (Fig. 15-6A). Such fasteners have a limited grip, but for a piece of furniture that stands on the floor or wherever the load on the fastening is not great, they are convenient.

Other fasteners use machine screws and are designed so that tightening the screw after the plug is inserted causes an expansion on the other side of the panel and prevents withdrawal (Fig. 15-6B).

Another device for fixing to hollow walls uses toggles. The hole has to be large enough to pass the toggle and so is larger than the bolt diameter (Fig. 15-6C). A washer is thus needed under the bolt head.

One form of toggle bolt has two spring-loaded arms for the toggle. The arms are pushed through the hole far enough to open then the screw is tightened to pull back against the panel (Fig. 15-6D).

Instead of having a spring, a wing may be weighted or arranged off center (Fig. 15-6E) so gravity causes the inserted assembly to open correctly. There may be prongs on the toggle to grip the wall panel. This allows removal and replacement of the bolt without the toggle dropping away.

The bolt does not always go into the toggle. It is sometimes more convenient to have a threaded rod pivoting on a wing and to make the attachment with a nut (Fig. 15-6F).

Fig. 15-6. Fastenings for fixing furniture to thin paneling include expanding plugs (A and B) and various types of toggle bolts (C through F).

LOCATING FASTENERS

How many fasteners to use depends on many factors. Much depends on the material to which attachment must be made. Sometimes an attachment does not have the security expected and additional ones have to be made. There should never be less than two fastenings. In the case of a hanging bookcase. two well spread fastenings near the top may be all that are needed. Even then it may be better to have more to spread the load on a lightly built hollow wall. For larger pieces of furniture, more fixings are needed, particularly up high.

How many to use must finally come down to experience, but a spacing of about every foot near the top and every 2 feet near the bottom is reasonable.

Some thought must be given to whether the furniture itself can hold the fixing screws. A piece of plywood or hardboard that forms a back or side panel is not adequate in itself. The screws should go through a strip of solid wood that is part of the framework and properly jointed to other parts.

PLATES

Putting a screw through an inch or so of wood is not always easy, particularly if holes have to be made, and plugs inserted, in an awkward place inside a cabinet. In some situations it is preferable to use a metal plate and fix through that. This may be allowed for and built into the furniture, possible with the plate screwed to a structural part but arranged over a thin panel which is easily accessible (Fig. 15-7A).

Mirror plates (Fig. 15-7B) are examples of plate mounting which can be made or bought. The name indicates their original use. Two holes are used to screw to the back of the mirror's frame, then the fastening to the wall is made through the remaining hole. For a thing like a bookcase the plates can be arranged less obviously inwards from the sides (Fig. 15-7C).

An alternative that keeps the plate hidden is to make it from thin brass or other metal and give it a double bend. The bending can be done in a vise. After the first bend, a strip of metal is used as a punch to knock the plate back (Fig. 15-7D). There are two screw holes in one arm and a keyhole slot in the other, the latter to hook over a flat-head screw projecting from the wall (Fig. 15-7E). Of course, this allows the mirror or other fitting to be removed conveniently for cleaning.

CABINET FITTINGS

There are a great many fittings for cabinetwork that are suitable for built-in furniture. There is little standardization, and the range of fittings available in one place may be different from those elsewhere. As some of these things—

Fig. 15-7. Mounting plates may be bought or made. They can be hidden (A through C) when used for fixing to a wall. A plate with a keyhole slot and a jog can be hidden, yet it allows the furniture to lift off (D and E).

special hinges, catches for doors, brackets for flaps, and many other things—are designed for wood of certain thicknesses or for particular movements. it is advisable to check on the availability of suitable fittings before getting too far into the design and construction of a piece of furniture. This will be much better than trying to alter something already made to suit the only available fittings.

Hinges

Ordinary hinges are dealt with in Chapter 11, and these should be used in any piece of built-in furniture of traditional pattern. For modern applications there are now hundreds of different styles available. If there is a special hinge problem in a piece of furniture. the available types should be checked before going ahead with the work.

If a door is to overlap. it can have a *cranked* hinge (Fig. 15-8A). These can be bought plated and with decorative outline shapes. and they are attractive on kitchen and bathroom cabinets. Some of the thickness of a butt hinge can be removed by making the two parts so one fits into a space in the other (Fig. 15-8B). The whole hinge is then probably no thicker than the clearance that will be given the door, and there is no need to recess it. There are also *cranked flush* hinges (Fig. 15-8C). A *double-cranked flush* hinge throws the door clear (Fig. 15-8D).

Fig. 15-8. Hinge types: cranked (A), butt (B), cranked flush (C), double-cranked flush (D); the hidden hinge (E) is a neat arrangement for folding doors (F). Twin hinges (G) are needed for hanging two doors from a central stile.

There are many hinges that seem to trace their ancestry to car doors, where linkage is used to swing the door clear as it opens. Some of these seem unnecessarily complicated for most built-in furniture, but if there is a need for a door to swing around an obstruction, there is probably a hinge made that will do it.

In some modern furniture the hinges are hidden when the door or lid is closed. In one type the two halves are circular and fit into holes (Fig. 15-8E). The hinges have a locking arranged to keep them in the holes. These hinges can be used to make neat folding doors (Fig. 15-8F).

If you want to hang two doors from a central stile, there are twin hinges (Fig. 15-8G). The central tongue fits into a slot. The doors may open to 90° together, or one door may swing fully back over the other closed one.

Catches

Doors and lids have to be fastened and they need handles. Sometimes the means of fastening is incorporated in a handle. What is used depends on the piece of furniture. There are styles applicable to traditional, colonial, and modern pieces.

Magnetic catches are convenient, as they need no action other than a pull to release. They are in several forms, but all incorporate on one part and a magnet and iron plate to attract it on the other part (Fig. 15-9A).

Another catch uses a roller under spring pressure (Fig. 15-9B). Related to these are the ball catches (Fig. 15-9C and D).

Fig. 15-9. Catches for doors and lids: magnetic catch (A), roller catch (B), ball catches (C and D).

A common construction in built-in furniture is a *fall front*, which serves as a writing surface or a kitchen working surface. Although two or more ordinary hinges could be used, this is a place for a piano hinge—a continuous length of hinge which is cut to length and screwed at intervals.

The fall front has to be supported in some way. In some traditional furniture there were pullout supports below, but it is more usual to have stays. There is an arm with a bracket to fix to the flap, and the other end is on a slide. At the bottom of the slide its movement is stopped at the point where the flap has reached the correct position (Fig. 15-10). There are many variations on this principle.

Fig. 15-10. Slide support for a fall front.

Handles

Handles for cabinetwork come in an infinite number of patterns in wood, metal, and plastic. A handle may be fastened from the front (Fig. 15-11A) or back (Fig. 15-11B). A drawer pull differs from a door pull by usually allowing for the fingers going underneath (Fig. 15-11C). Other handles may go on the edge (Fig. 15-11D). Sometimes handles may be dispensed with by providing holes or notches (Fig. 15-11E). A further step is an inset metal finger-pull (Fig. 15-11F).

Period furniture can generate ideas for many knobs and handles; there are also many modern designs. Care is needed to look at anything in relation to what will be around it. Handles have to be compatible with their surroundings.

There is much to be said for making your own handles. If you have a lathe, turned knobs are interesting projects. Handles do not have to be very ornate. Drawer pulls can be made in a long piece and cut off (Fig. 15-11G). Door handles can be made in a similar way. If the same wood as the rest of

Fig. 15-11. Handles may fix from front or back or go along an edge (A through D). Notching an edge may take the place of a handle (E) or there may be a flush pull (F). Handles may be produced in a strip (G).

the construction is used and it is felt that some color is needed, a piece of Plexiglass can be included under the handle (Fig. 15-12). This will also prevent the wood from becoming soiled.

Other Fittings

Although the enthusiastic woodworker will want to make and fit drawers by traditional methods, there are several drawer slide assemblies that can be obtained. They often give a smoother action than wood sliding on wood, and some give a much better support when the drawer is fully drawn.

Doors do not always have to swing; it may be more convenient to have them slide. There are several types of sliding-door gear in cabinet sizes. If one is to be used, it should be bought first so the piece of furniture can be designed to suit it.

Fig. 15-12. A polished wooden handle with a piece of dark plastic behind it to protect the paint and improve the appearance. Fastening is by screws from the other side of the door.

Though proper cabinetmaking joints should always be used where possible. there are places where reinforcement may be advisable or where a simple piece of hardware could give added strength to a joint. This sometimes happens when more than two pieces of wood meet in one place and the joint cut results in quite a lot of wood being removed from each piece. There are flat plates (Fig. 15-13A) and corner plates (Fig. 15-13B). Others are shaped like brackets to go around inside or outside of corners (Fig. 15-13C).

Fig. 15-13. There are several standard metal reinforcing plates (A through C) besides shelf brackets (D).

Shelves may be supported in other parts of the woodwork at their ends. but if intermediate supports are needed or the shelf has to be supported without benefit of framing, metal shelf brackets (Fig. 15-13D) are neater and less obvious than any wooden brackets. For where there is a possibility the shelves will have to be moved. there are adjustable brackets.

Upholstery

Not many built-in pieces of furniture require upholstery, but such things as window seats and seats built into recesses may be better finished with something more than a wooden base and back. It may be possible to make the seat sufficiently comfortable with loose cushions, but with modern materials it is not difficult to provide something comparable with the padding and covering of an ordinary chair.

Traditional materials have been largely superseded by synthetic ones. The only snag with man-made materials is that they do not "breath." Consequently, prolonged use may cause dampness to accumulate under them. If a built-in seat is to have a piece of plywood or solid wood under upholstery or cushioning of synthetic material, it is best to perforate the wood. A piece of perforated hardboard could be used, but it is probably better to use somewhat larger holes in plywood (Fig. 16-1). A matte surface seems to attract less moisture than a glossy one. If the cushions are loose, they are less likely to slip on a matte surface.

If there is to be no resilience in the support, any cushioning needs to be at least 3 in. thick for a seat, 4 in. or more for greater comfort or sleeping. The alternative is to use a flexible support under thinner cushioning, usually in the form of webbing.

Fig. 16-1. The wood under a cushion of synthetic material in a built-in seat should be perforated.

WEBBING

The webbing may be a fabric type with strips 1½ in. or wider and with only minimal stretch, or a rubberized type that possesses some elasticity. The first is traditional, but the other is used where the seat is expected to conform more to body shape.

Whichever type is used, it is usual to interweave it on a wooden frame of sufficient stiffness (Fig. 16-2). The closeness of weave depends on the strength required and the density of what goes above. A rather loosely made cushion would need a relatively close weave of webbing.

Fig. 16-2. The alternative to a perforated cushion support is webbing interwoven on a sturdy wooden frame.

It is difficult to get sufficient tension by hand and to control the strain while fastening the webbing, so a strainer should be made or bought (Fig. 16-3A). Sizes are suggested in the accompanying illustration, but these could be adapted to suit available material. The webbing is looped around a rod to hold it for tightening. The rod can be a piece of doweling, or almost any scrap piece of wood, not necessarily round.

Webbing is usually fastened with tacks or large-head nails. At one side a little surplus webbing is allowed to extend, then three tacks are driven (Fig. 6-3B). The surplus piece is turned over, and three more tacks are driven. With a woven webbing, the end should be turned under to prevent fraying.

The strainer should have a beveled or rounded end. This is placed against the frame at the opposite side, the webbing is dipped through the slot and the peg is inserted. The excess webbing is gripped by the hand (Fig. 16-3D). Levering downward tensions the webbing while the first three tacks are driven. It is important to keep about the same tension on each length of webbing, otherwise the seat may settle unevenly after prolonged use.

PADDING

Various forms of foam rubber and plastic may be obtained, either in pieces to cut to size or in cushion shapes. With some forms of built-in seats or beds, it may be advisable at the planning stage to check on the available sizes of upholstery padding and arrange the other work accordingly. An advantage of using a stock size is that the ends as well as the surface will be in a smooth-finished form, usually with rounded corners. However, if the best rounded edge that can be achieved with knife or scissors is not as uniform as you wish, the covering material can probably coax it into an acceptable curve.

Where furniture has inaccessible parts, as most built-in furniture will, it is usually best to arrange the upholstered parts to lift out. If cushions are bought, they may be merely placed in position; but it is more usual to have to make up something to fit the available space.

CUSHIONS AND BASES

The making of cushions is outside the scope of this book, but a few hints about cushions are in order. It is probably best to cover the rubber or plastic lining with one or more layers of cloth, then make a removable cover from material that matches the other furniture. The buttons or other fasteners are arranged along what will be the rear edge. The cushion need

Fig. 16-3. A strainer (A) is needed to make each strip of webbing taut; six tacks are used at the ends of the strips (B and C). Using the edge of the frame as a fulcrum, the strainer is levered downward to tension the webbing (D).

not be a rounded form, but a block of foam with squared edges and slightly rounded angles can be covered so it is a close fit into the available space. A long seat may be covered better with several sections of cushion than with one long one.

If a rigid base for the upholstery is desired, the base can be plywood, which is arranged to lift out. A box seat in a recess may have a lip at the front so that the complete upholstered top is located but can be removed to give access to the interior (Fig. 16-4A). Depending on size, the base may be thin plywood with a frame (Fig. 16-4B), or for more rigidity it could be thicker plywood or blockboard, with or without framing (Fig. 16-4C).

COVERING THE FURNITURE

The buttons on upholstery often are not just decorative. They prevent the covering and filling from moving in relation to each other. This is essential for anything except the smallest assembly.

With framed plywood the foam is located on the base, then the lining cloth is fitted over it and turned underneath. Fix it with tacks around the edge. Probably every 3 in. will be sufficient. Use only enough tension to bring the cloth into close contact with the foam (Fig. 16-4D). If the cloth edge will not be covered, turn under the cut edge to prevent fraying. If the underside is to be covered, put this on and bring it up around the sides (Fig. 16-4E). If the box is to be used for storing blankets or bedding, a cloth lining for the lid is desirable.

The ease of fitting the outer covering material depends on its type. A loosely woven fabric is amenable to pulling into shape, but imitation leather, which is a plastic coating on a fabric backing, has little stretch and needs careful manipulation. It may be necessary to do some work over.

Stretch the covering material over the area to be covered and tack along opposite sides first, then do the other sides, pleating the corners neatly. You may fix the material with round-head or decorative upholstery nails (Fig. 16-4F). Or you may use a row of plain tacks and cover these with a strip of gimp (trimming) braid (Fig. 16-4G).

Holes for the thread and buttons are probably best drilled in the wood base before assembly. If is usual to arrange them so a pattern is formed. Their spacing depends on the materials used. The stiffer coverings do not need as many as the more flexible materials, but more may be used for the sake of appearance.

There are upholstery buttons that can be covered with the same material as the covering. Alternatively, any button with a loop on the back may be used on the surface (Fig. 16-4H). Underneath, an ordinary 2-hole coat button can be used (Fig. 16-4I). If a flush finish is wanted a wooden or wire pin may be allowed to spring into a slot (Fig. 16-4J), where it is hidden by the cloth lining. Use a stout thread, as breakages in use could be a nuisance. Carpet and sailmaking thread are suitable.

Fig. 16-4. The upholstered part of a built-in seat may lift out (A), but most modern upholstery uses a rubber or plastic foarm insert, which is covered by material and held with buttons at intervals (B through L).

Most synthetic threads are stronger size for size than natural fiber threads and will not rot.

There are special long upholsterer's needles, some of them pointed at both ends. but any needle long enough to reach through will do. Put on several turns of thread, then tension as required before tying under the bottom button (Fig. 16-4K). One advantage of using a pin instead of a button is that is can be used to twist the thread to adjust tension. However, too much reliance should not be put on this, as turning of the top button will eventually alter the tension.

If the inside would benefit by some padding—as when storage is to be provided for clothing, drapes, or linen—thin foam plastic may be fixed with adhesive to hardboard (or even card); then this is covered with lining cloth, which is turned under and tacked through (Fig. 16-4L). Adhesive may be used on the cloth edge before tacking.

Designs And Preparations

With free-standing furniture there are plenty of designs available in magazines and books, with all sizes given and with step-by-step instructions and ample illustrations. With built-in furniture each item must usually be of an individual design, particularly if it is to fit into a recess or occupy a certain position on a wall. Although there may be instructions available based on how someone else did a job, these will almost certainly have to be modified to suit your needs. This means that anyone making built-in furniture needs to know a little about design so he can adapt a pattern that appeals to him or so he can originate his own design to suit his needs.

DESIGN FEATURES

There are two main considerations in design: utility and appearance. There is no use making something pleasing to look at if it is unsuitable for its intended purpose. Similarly, it is displeasing to make something that fulfills its purpose but is ugly. Fortunately, fitness for purpose usually results in a pleasing design.

It is useful to consider the article to be made in relation to an average person. Assume a piece of furniture has working and storage areas. For standing, a reasonable work height is about 36 in. (Fig. 17-1A). For sitting, the work height is better at about 30 in., with a seat level of about 17 in.

Storage Items

For storage, the most convenient height for handling items, particularly if the items are heavy, is between waist and shoulder height, with a slight reach upward being preferable to much of a bend downward (Fig. 17-1B). Heavy-item storage levels should be between 36 and 72 in. or so (Fig. 17-1C).

Fig. 17-1. Spatial considerations in design. Parts must be planned to hold what is intended and must be within reach.

If the furniture is not a working item like a kitchen cabinet or desk, it does not matter how the bottom is arranged; but if anyone is to stand facing the furniture, the bottom should be cut back (Fig. 17-1D) to give toe clearance and reduce damage from kicking.

If the furniture is for storage only, it will probably be made as deep as a recess will allow, or it will be extended from a wall as far as possible without interfering with the use of the room. If it is to be a working item, a back-to-front distance of not more than 24 in. is advisable, otherwise reaching to the back may be too much of an effort. If it is a clothes closet, about 22 in. should be allowed for the width of coats on hangers. If the width has to be less than this, the coats will have to hang diagonally (Fig. 17-1E), which reduces capacity.

Handles and Hinges

The positions of handles and pulls will have to be related to other design features, but if there is a full-depth door, the handle should be at the same height as room doors, or about 36 in., so it can be reached without bending. For smaller doors a handle at exactly center height does not look as good as one above or below that—especially above. Drawer pulls look better and are more functional if placed above the center line (Fig. 17-2A).

Hinges on a door always look better if the space from the top is less than the space from the bottom (Fig. 17-2B). If both distances are the same, the lower distance looks less. How to space two drawer pulls cannot be settled geometrically, but one-quarter of the drawer width from each end is about right (Fig. 17-2C).

Shapes

Getting shapes that are pleasing depends to a certain extent on the designer's artistic ability, and this often comes with experience. However, there are a few pointers that help in arriving at satisfactory shapes. For most things the predominant lines should be horizontal and vertical. Diagonal lines are best avoided. There are occasions when diagonals can be introduced, but normally they should have a secondary effect.

Fig. 17-2. The appearance of built-in cabinets and cupboards is always better if handles are above the center line (A), and hinge lower spaces are greater than higher ones (B). A rule of thumb for locating drawer pulls is to center them at one-quarter drawer width within the drawer edge (C).

Exact squares are best avoided. A rectangle is much better. particularly a length about 1½ items the width (Fig. 17-3A). If one rectangle comes inside another, it is better to keep the border fairly narrow (Fig. 17-3B). With the border exactly the same all around, the border at the bottom always looks narrower. so it is usual to make this wider (Fig. 17-3C). If you want something to appear tall or slim. include plenty of vertical lines (Fig. 17-3D). If you want it to appear broad or flat. use horizontal lines (Fig. 17-3E).

It seems more natural to use a heavier construction down low. so framing may be wider. where it is visible, near the bottom of a cabinet than higher up. In a two-part construction, such as a storage cupboard below and a display cabinet above, let widths of visible parts on the top part be narrower than those in the lower part. This need for any heavy appearance to

Fig. 17-3. In furniture, rectangles look better than squares, narrow borders are usually better than wide ones, and ellipses look better than circles. Vertical lines make heights seem greater, and horizontal lines make widths seem greater.

seem low is also true with colors. If you are mixing woods or using different paints, let the lower part be darker than the higher part.

In much modern furniture it is better to keep to straight lines, but if curves are used a ellipse is better than a circle (Fig. 17-3F). Part of an ellipse is better than part of a circle for a cutout corner (Fig. 17-4A). Even with small things like the edge of a flap or table, an elliptical curve (Fig. 17-4B) looks better than a circular one (Fig. 17-4C).

Fig. 17-4. Minor curves that are parts of ellipses look better than arcs of circles.

Drawings

It is helpful to make a drawing. This does not have to be in great detail. Choose a convenient scale and get the main outlines down in something like the correct proportions, at first in light lines. Then go over the lines representing the edges of framing, drawers, doors, and other prominent features so they show up clearly. You will soon see if the result is what you want and likely to look satisfactory. If there are other nearby features in the room that will affect the final appearance, sketch them in to approximately scale. Stand back and look at the drawing propped up vertically. This is much better than viewing close to a drawing flat on a table.

MATING SURFACES

One thing that soon becomes apparent is that many homes lack precision in their construction. A home may be just as comfortable to live in with a corner at 85° instead of 90° and with a wall that has a slight curve and is not vertical, but problems come when furniture has to be made to match.

Although the edges of furniture may have to be made to match any irregularities, it is important that paneling, doors, shelves, windows, and all the normally visible construction should be horizontal and vertical, rather than parallel to inaccurate surfaces. Any lack of squareness in these items will be very obvious.

Checking Levelness

A floor should be tested with a level (Fig. 17-5A). If the floor is very unlevel, it may be wiser to ignore it as a means of checking levels and use a false bottom as a base for measuring from, adding a plinth outside to disguise discrepancies (Fig. 17-5B). In some furniture it may be better to establish a horizontal surface at a higher level and use this as a reference for other surfaces. This could be a shelf or other salient level surface (Fig. 17-5C). With one horizontal surface established, other surfaces should be checked from it for levelness. The carpenter's level can provide a second check.

Fig. 17-5. If the floor is checked with a level (A) and it is found to be way out of kilter, use a plinth under the furniture (B) to correct the fault. It may be necessary to use a higher reference surface to check others (C).

Many levels will also check vertical surfaces. If the level is not very long, use a straightedge that reaches somewhere near the height of the furniture for testing. There may be minor irregularities in a wall, and a short level may follow these and indicate a lack of trueness where the overall reading would be different. This is especially likely with plastered surfaces.

Spiling

Lack of verticalness at the back of a cabinet may not be of much consequence, but if the side of a recess has a variable line, the adjoining edge of the piece of furniture will have to be shaped to fit. This outline can be obtained by *spiling* (Fig. 17-6A). A spiling piece—a strip of wood—is held vertically, then a block or wood and a pencil is used to follow the line of the wall surface at the back of the cabinet. A scrap piece of wood is then marked as a template. The spiling piece is put over it. then the block of wood is put against the pencil line, and the pencil is used against the block to reproduce the line of the wall on the template (Fig. 17-6B). The template is cut and tried against the wall. If necessary the edge can be adjusted to suit. then the template can be used to mark the cabinet edge. Of course. the template might be dispensed with and the cabinet marked directly from the spiling strip, but there is then a risk of losing verticalness of the other part of the cabinet wood if much adjusting has to be done to the edge.

It sometimes happens that the fitted furniture has to be cut around a base or picture molding. It may be simpler and better to cut this away so the furniture goes tight against the wall and the cut molding butts against it. but if there is a risk of damaging the wall in removing the molding. it may be better to leave the molding in place. If the built-in furniture may have to be removed at some later date. it is better to leave the wall and its molding undisturbed. In that case the molding shape can be obtained with a pointed spiling stick (Fig. 17-6C) and

Fig. 17-6. Spiling techniques for fitting furniture alongside a wavy wall (A and B) or against an existing molding (C and D).

174

reproduced on the template by connecting marks around the point (Fig. 17-6C). There are adjustable templates that can be used, but these are limited to only a few inches.

Checking Angles

When furniture is to go into a recess, it is important to check the angles of the corners. If the furniture is made right-angled and the corner is wider than a right angle, there will be a gap at the front (Fig. 17-17A). If the angle is less than a right angle but the furniture is right-angled, it may go in and look satisfactory if it has been made to measurements at the front; but if the measurements were taken at the back, it may be too big to fit.

For anything of no great width, such as bookshelves, the corner angle may be obtained with an adjustable bevel (Fig. 17-17B) and directly transfered to the shelf end (Fig. 17-7C). It

Fig. 17-7. A gap between the wall and the side of furniture in a corner can be avoided by first checking the corner angel with an adjustable bevel (B); the angle of the bevel can then be transfered to the furniture (C).

is always bad practice to extend anything short to suit anything long, and there would be too much risk of error to use this method for something much wider than the length of the bevel blade.

Convenient measurements can be taken in both directions from a corner, with one going at least as far as the furniture will reach. The distance Z between these points is then taken (Fig. 17-8A). If the base measurement is taken along an edge, and an arc with the other wall measurement is swung with rule or tape measure from one point (Fig. 17-8B), a measurement of the diagonal Z will locate a mark through which a line (see dashed line) can be drawn at the same angle to the edge Y as the angle of the corner.

For a two-sided recess, measurements can be made from opposite corners (Fig. 17-8C). Internal measurements may be taken with an expending tape rule, or two overlapping sticks

Fig. 17-8. Measurements for furniture that is to fit in a corner or alcove can be made with a tape, or with a overlapping strips to reproduce the same shapes on parts being fitted.

may be used, with their overlaps marked so they can be put together again at the same distance (Fig. 17-8D). For many assemblies, when there are errors in the walls, it is a good idea to use a piece of plywood as a template on which to base parts of the construction. The plywood can eventually be used for the top or some other part of the furniture.

Basic Built-Ins

Though a complex piece of multipurpose built-in furniture should be within the scope of most readers of this book, it is obviously better to start with something simpler. There are many basic built-in furniture items that are easy to make, yet fulfill a purpose and are satisfying to a craftsman.

RAILS FOR HANGING

On a wall that will not take such things as coat hooks or hangers for domestic tools directly, it is necessary to fasten a strip of wood to which these holders can be screwed. Even on a wall where direct fitting is possible, a piece of wood keeping the hanging items clear of the wall may be desirable. It may be decorated on the edges, either by molding or a simple chamfer (Fig. 18-1A). Corners should be taken off. For most situations it is advisable to have a trial assembly, then take down the board and paint it or stain and varnish it.

Leveling may be done by making the board parallel to the floor by measurement, but it is safer to use a level. The best way of ensuring accuracy is to fasten one end temporarily on a screw so the board can be swung level, then to mark through the position of the screw at the other end (Fig. 18-1B). If the board is long, intermediate holes can also be marked. Then the

Fig. 18-1. It is always best to back built-ins that will be nailed or screwed to a wall with a strip of wood (A), which should first be made true with a level (B).

strip is removed and wall plugs prepared before final fastening.

SOME SIMPLE SHELVES

Another simple project is the fixing of a single shelf, which can be solid wood, edged chipboard, or thin framed plywood. This may be mounted merely on brackets, but it is better to add a horizontal strip under the back edge to prevent a sag in the length. If this is done, there should be strips behind the brackets. The strips may be tenoned or halved into the crosswise strip before mounting on the wall (Fig. 18-2).

Fig. 18-2. There should be vertical support strips behind the brackets on a wall-mounted shelf.

Homemade Mounts

In many cases, metal shelf brackets will be used. The alternative is to make brackets of wood. For a utilitarian shelf (Fig. 18-3), in which a functional appearance is all that is

Fig. 18-3. Brackets with notched struts support a small table. Note the stiffening piece under the front to prevent the plywood top from warping. The piece across the back prevents things on the table from marking the wall.

needed, brackets can be built up with struts notched in place (Fig. 18-4A). A single dovetail at the back resists the forward-pulling load of the shelf (Fig. 18-4B). There is a tendency for a shelf to settle, even on metal brackets, and develop a slight slope forward. In any case, a shelf that is truly level, back to front, appears to be lower toward the front. Because of this it is always a good idea to make the front edge of any shelf very slightly higher than the back.

Where the bracket is to be more decorative, solid wood can be used and the edge shaped (Fig. 18-4C). Fixing is done with screws or dovetailed dado joints. The whole thing is made as a complete assembly before fixing to the wall. A small shelf with a single bracket can be purely functional, as in Fig. 18-5, or something more elaborate.

If the shelf is to hold a potted plant or something else that is not fixed down, it may be advisable to put a rim around the shelf top. It is usually better not to make this continuous. If the rim is made in sections, as shown in Fig. 18-4D, the shelf will be easier to clean.

Fig. 18-4. The brackets for a utilitarian shelf can be struts notched in place (A) a single dovetail at the back (B) will resist stress. For a more decorative appearance the strut can be shaped (C). Interrupted rim makes cleaning easier (D).

If a shelf is to fit in a corner or recess, there may be a ledger under the end of the shelf (Fig. 18-6). If the ledger will show, it may stop a short distance from the front edge of the shelf and be given a beveled end. Exposed edges should be chamfered. If the shelf is in a recess, it may be advisable to fix

Fig. 18-5. A small shelf covers a joint in the hardboard paneling of a utility room. Its wooden bracket has a more graceful appearance than the standard metal shelf bracket.

one ledger, then use the shelf or a piece of scrap wood with a level to get the exact height of the other ledger. Similarly, if one edge of the shelf will rest on a ledger and the other end on a bracket, fix the ledger first, and get the position of the bracket by using a level.

Fig. 18-6. Ledgers are used under shelves butted against nearby walls.

If there are already horizontal strips of wood on a wall, it may be possible to use them as supports for a shelf or part of a cabinet. However, their security should be checked first. If they are just decorative or are there to cover the edge of a wall panel, for instance, the original mounting may not have been intended for load bearing. It may be necessary to add other fastenings in the area where the new load is to come.

Triangular Shelf

In a corner, a simple triangle of plywood will make a shelf. It may be edged to give a better appearance, and anything but the smallest shelf ought to have a stiffener below (Fig. 18-7A). The stiffener and edging could be one piece, and this could be taken above the surface to prevent anything from rolling off (Fig. 18-7B).

A simple triangle does not provide much shelf area in relation to its size. This can be increased by cutting the ends of the front edge perpendicular to the wall (Fig. 18-7C) but this should not be carried too far, or there may be sagging.

CORNER CLOTHES CLOSET

The triangular-shelf idea can be used to make a simple corner clothes closet supported on existing strips on the walls (Fig. 18-8). Such an arrangement does not have a great capacity, because of its triangular shape, but if it is allowed to

Fig. 18-7. A triangular corner shelf (A) should have a stiffener (B) below it. Its surface can be extended for more room (C), as long as it's structurally sound to do so.

come far enough forward, there can be hooks on the wall, as well as a central rail to take coat hangers (Fig. 18-9A).

The top piece may be a piece of plywood, blockboard, or hardboard. Glue and nails may be adequate for the framing, which will not be visible, although mortise-and-tenon joints may be used. The plywood may be recessed into grooves. The front is a strip deep enough to take a curtain rail, mitered or notched to make a neat fit at the ends, with an overhanging piece to give an appearance of solidity (Fig. 18-9B).

The rail can be a bought metal one, or a piece of dowel rod between blocks can be used. If thin plywood is used for the top, there should be a stiffening piece as well (Fig. 18-9C). Blocks can be taken through and tenoned to this piece, or screws may be sufficient. If there are to be hooks on the wall, these can be fixed to the existing rail if it is wide enough; otherwise, new pieces should be fixed below the rail.

Curtains to the closet may reach the floor. If there is space left below the clothing, there may be a shelf built in for shoes or other things. Rails should be made with dowel rods (Fig. 18-9D).

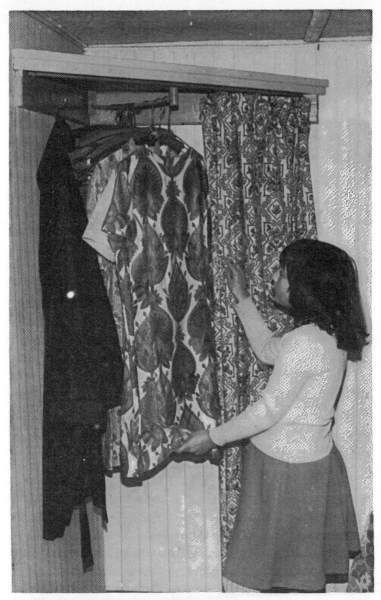

Fig. 18-8. A triangle of plywood with a stiffened front edge makes a simple clothes closet in the corner of a room.

BASIC BOOKCASE

A simple bookcase for a flat wall is an example of a typical built-in furniture assembly. The bookcase could have several

Fig. 18-9. Construction details of the corner clothes closet in Fig. 18-8.

front

rail

dowel rod

shelves, but the example (Fig. 18-10) assumes only one row of books.

Prepare all wood to size. Plane all around and leave a little extra on the length. Cut rabbets for the plywood in the two end pieces (Fig. 18-10A). Mark the pieces together (to ensure that they match) with overall length and the positions of the shelves. Cut off the bottom ends slightly outside the lines. Cut the dado joint at the top (Fig. 18-10B).

Mark the two shelves and the top (together) with the thickness of the end pieces. The bottom shelf will go right through the ends with dovetails. The other two horizontal pieces will be shorter, but the lines indicating the inner surfaces of the end pieces will ensure cutting so the parts match (Fig. 18-10C). The curve of the top edge can be drawn with pencil by springing a flexible piece of wood through the end points and a central one at the right height (Fig. 18-10D).

Cut the dado joints in the end pieces. If these are to be made by hand, chop out the front stopped parts and saw into these before removing the waste between the saw cuts with a chisel or router (Fig. 18-10E). Cut the top shelf to length, and notch the front edge. For the sake of appearance this should be a clean, tight joint, so cut the lines with a knife before sawing. It may be advisable to bevel with a chisel to start the fine backsaw accurately (Fig. 18-10F).

Open the rabbet at the back, above the shelf line, to take the thickness of the back piece (Fig. 18-10G). Cut that piece to length and shape its top. Complete the tops of the ends.

For the dovetail joints at the bottom, the tails should be in the sides and the pins on the bottom. To cover the plywood back, there is a half dovetail. This simplifies marking, as a reasonable spacing for the ordinary dovetails can be made and any surplus taken up at the back edge. At each joint have the wood a little long (less than $\frac{1}{16}$ in.) in both directions. This allows for planing level after the joint has been made. But if too much is left on, there is difficulty in cutting the waste out between dovetails and pins.

cut outside line

back

shelves

Fig. 18-10. A hanging bookcase is an example of the application of traditional methods of construction.

185

Fig. 18-11. The dado joints can be reinforced with screws going in from below.

Clean up the surfaces that will be difficult to get at after assembly. If necessary, use a smoothing plane, then thoroughly sand anything that will be inaccessible. It is worthwhile strengthening the dado joints with screws from below—one at the front at each end, and another farther back if the joint is wide (Fig. 18-11). Drill the shelf ends before assembly.

Excess glue can be a nuisance to remove cleanly, and it may show through a transparent finish. It is, therefore, important to get sufficient glue in a joint for strength, but not so much that it squeezes out as the joint is pulled together.

Although it may be possible to assemble the bookcase without using clamps, it is helpful to have bar clamps. In any case, put glue in all joints, assemble the lengthwise pieces to one end, and then add the other end. If no clamps are used, put a piece of scrap wood over one end and drive the parts together with a mallet or hammer.

If bar clamps are used, have scrap pieces of wood ready, each as long as the width of the ends and with smooth surfaces to contact the bookcase. If the scrap wood is softer than the wood used in the bookcase, there is little risk of the bookcase being marked when pressure is applied. Put one clamp at the bottom, but locate the scrap pieces above the dovetail joint so the slightly overlength pins are not prevented from going through. Put the other clamp at the top. Attach the back with screws into the ends. The glued joint between it and the top shelf may be adequate, but if there is any tendency to spring, drive one or two screws from below.

Check squareness by measuring diagonals. Before the glue has set in the joints, cut the plywood back to size, with the ends carefully squared. Put this in place with glue in the rabbets and behind the shelves, and fix it with small nails at about 2 or 3 in. intervals. Attaching the back should square up the assembly, but check diagonals at the front to make sure. Leave the assembly front downward on a flat surface for the glue to set. This will reduce any risk of a twist developing.

When the glue has set, remove any surplus inside and plane the dovetail joints. Remove any sharp edges and give the whole bookcase a thorough sanding before finishing.

Fig. 18-12. Screws in the joints between the bookcase ends and the top shelf will counteract any tendency to spring.

How the bookcase is hung will depend on its size, but for all but the largest, it will probably be sufficient to put two screws through the top piece, where it fits into the ends. The weight of the case and its load of books should keep the piece close to the wall, but for a large bookcase, there may be additional screws through the plywood back, lower down. If necessary, use reinforcing metal plates fixed to the sides to take some of the load from the plywood.

The principles outlined for this simple bookcase can be used in many other pieces of furniture which depend on hanging from the wall. Horizontal members that come under load should be joined to upright members in a way that resists the downward pressure of the load. Attachment comes near the top so that the lower part presses towards the wall when the item is hanging. As the top is to take the load, attachments are arranged there through a stout piece of wood, and this is fixed to the ends or other parts in a way that transfers the load. Lower parts of the back, which do not have to share much of the hanging load, may be plywood or hardboard. If the piece of furniture is large and fastenings have to be arranged elsewhere besides the top, there should be other stout crossbars or metal plates arranged so the load is taken by something besides the plywood back.

Fitting As You Go

Much built-in furniture can be prefabricated to a large extent before it is fitted. In general it is easier and more accurate to do as much as possible on the bench before bringing the furniture to the location for final fitting. This should be done whenever possible.

Sometimes. however. it is necessary to fit the furniture as you go. Room surfaces and angles may be inaccurate and variable.

Doors or windows must function. yet the best use of the furniture will be obtained by not letting the clearance around them be any more than necessary. There may be some sort of kitchen appliance or a floor-standing power tool that furniture has to be built around without much tolerance for error. In these circumstances the best approach is to build up most of the furniture structure a piece at a time. on locations. Things like doors and drawers may be made on the bench, but the main structural parts to which they fit are assembled in place.

PLANNING THE WORK

Building furniture in this way is easy enough if the work is thought out in advance. Chalk marks can be made on walls and floor to indicate outlines. either approximate or final. If they

Fig. 19-1. An example of a purpose-built kitchen cabinet; this one fills a corner space and allows movement of a sliding door.

are final lines, check that they are horizontal and vertical with a level or other tool, even if the surfaces they are on are out of true. Whatever the shape of the recess or other house structure, a new piece of furniture built in has to have a level top surface, a vertical front, and properly squared corners and joints. It is always bad practice to match an untrue surface by making new work inaccurate.

A rough sketch is advisable to see if what is planned is feasible. It may be advisable to make a mock up of old plywood, hardboard, or card, particularly if the shape is awkward or there is a close-fitting article to be accommodated. The saying "Measure twice before cutting once" can be expanded to include modeling before cutting.

KITCHEN STORAGE UNIT

If there is an awkward part to the structure, it may be advisable to deal with this first. An example is where a unit has to allow a sliding door to run into it. A block of curved shelves reduces any obstruction to the doorway (Fig. 19-1A) yet allows the unit to be carried as far as possible and give maximum storage. At the other end the unit may be carried a short distance around a corner to come against the side of a refrigerator and gain a few extra inches of storage space (Fig. 19-1B). If the corner is out of square and the plastered walls uneven, this is the sort of kitchen storage cabinet and worktop (Fig. 19-2) that can only be successfully made in position.

Structural Parts

In the example a top rail is screwed and plugged to the wall (Fig. 19-3A). If kept less than 1 in. thick, it is sufficiently flexible to follow the slightly uneven wall surface. Joints are cut for crossmembers before the piece is fixed. There is an upright wide enough to give clearance to the door (Fig. 19-3B) and an assembly made on a piece of plywood that will be fixed to it (Fig. 19-3C and Fig. 19-4). This assembly may need testing and trying in position several times before it fits and floor and has an upright front edge.

The shelves are completely made and fixed before this subunit is finally put in position. A certain amount of fitting of

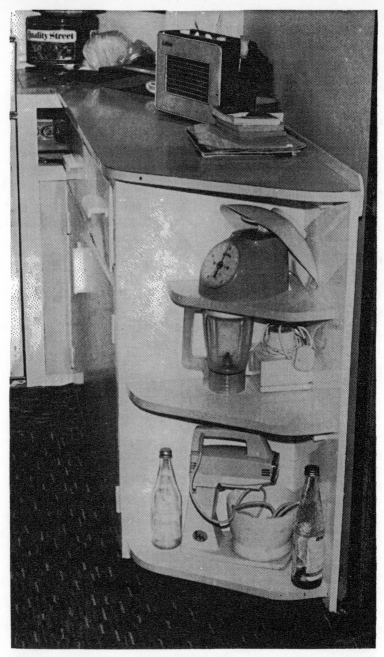

Fig. 19-2. In this kitchen cabinet, the shaped end allows easy access to the doorway, and the angle at the other end makes maximum use of available space.

Fig. 19-3. The kitchen cabinet is based on strips fixed to the wall (A and B), and a section built outward, on which other parts are based (C).

the front-door stile, drawer runners, shelf supports, and any top framing, can be done. All of these pieces may have joints cut ready to take other parts. Any joint cutting in this way is easier done as the wood is prepared on the bench than after it is fixed in position.

The shelf—door—end assembly should be tested vertically, and it should be at a right angle to the front of the cabinet (Fig. 19-5A), even if it is not at a right angle to the wall. This assembly and the top rail along the wall provide references from which other parts are measured.

Continue the lines of the top and any shelves around the walls (Fig. 19-5B) with suitable strips. Although the example goes around a corner a short distance, let the front top support go right through, and allow for the extension to be joined to it.

The extension can be framed plywood (Fig. 19-5C). See that it stands upright and has an upright front edge, even if the rear edge has to be shaped to an uneven wall. Screw to the wall and the floor. Build in short pieces as necessary to support any shelving.

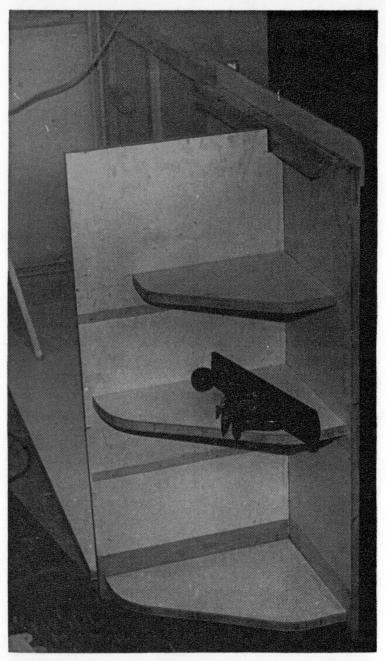

Fig. 19-4. An early stage in making the kitchen unit, with some framing fixed to the wall and the end assembly being used as a guide to making and fitting other parts.

Fig. 19-5. When the first part has been checked for accuracy (A), other parts are built onto it (B and C).

Do not be in a hurry to fit the top. It may be helpful to cut the material used for the top at this stage to try in position, but leave its actual fitting until all of the internal work has been done. If the wall is out of true, leave some surplus material at the front of the top until the rear edges have been planed to match the wall, then trim the exposed edges to come parallel to the parts of the front framing they overlap.

Fig. 19-6. The cabinet corner near the refrigerator is just wide enough to let the door clear the refrigerator front.

Drawers and Doors

In the example there are two drawers under the top, and the rest is storage space with a pair of doors. The corner by the

Fig. 19-7. Drawers fit into guides (A) and have overlapping fronts (B and C). The shelf, which has a thickened front (D), is in three pieces (E).

refrigerator is made wide enough for the door to swing clear of the refrigerator front, but not any more than necessary, as any excess width makes it more difficult to reach behind the extension. Here is another reason for building up a little at a time in position (Fig. 19-6).

The drawers are given runners and kickers (Fig. 19-7A). They could be made in several ways, but they are shown with rabbet and dado joints (Fig. 19-7B). False fronts cover the openings and disguise any slight discrepancies, as well as serving as dust shields (Fig. 19-7C).

The shelf has a thickened front and is stiffened (Fig. 19-7D). Because of difficulty in fitting a single piece of plywood accurately, it is in three pieces: one across the extended end, and the other two meeting on a rail at the doorpost (Fig. 19-7E).

The doors are made to match the openings. These should be square and true, but at this stage the doors must match, even if there are slight inaccuracies in the framing. The bottom of the door could be level with the bottom shelf to allow heavy items to be moved in and out and sweeping to be done easily. If the floor is very uneven or otherwise unsuitable to form the bottom of the unit, there must be framing to support a piece of plywood used as a false bottom.

The flush-mounted doors are made of plywood or hardboard panels on strip wood. Make a panel for each door with sufficient clearance. Pencil a mark on each panel and an adjoining part of the framing so it will be returned the same way. Use these pieces to mark the other panels, which may be left a little oversize until after fixing. The strips are best mitered at the top corners, but this is unnecessary at the bottom, where the joints will not show (Fig. 19-8A). Fix the strips to the first plywood panels with glue and fine nails. If the panels seem to flex too much, put an extra strip across the center (Fig. 19-8B). Glue on the opposite panels. When the glue has set, plane the edges true, using the shapes of the first panels as guides. Fit hinges, catches, and handles to complete the doors.

How the top is mounted will depend on its type. If it is to be covered with Formica, screws may be driven from above in counterbored holes. which are then plugged (Fig. 19-8C). Otherwise screw from below through thinner parts of the framing and use pocket screws (Fig. 19-8D) or blocks (Fig. 19-8E) at other places.

When such a cabinet has had to be shaped to match a wall with an uneven surface, meeting edges look better if covered. In a kitchen or bathroom there may be tiles. A strip of wood with a molded edge can be used (Fig. 19-8F), or there may be a length of plastic or metal molding.

Fig. 19-8. The cabinet shelves and doors are built-up pieces (A and B). The plastic-covered top may be fixed from above or below (C through E). A wall molding may be attached (F).

CONCLUSION

In any similar situation where building in position is the method used. it is well to establish a long horizontal member and an end part or division projecting from it to serve as the reference from which other parts are planned. Always check that anything that comes to a front or other exposed edge is upright and that openings are at right angles. Apart from the use of testing tools. standing back as far as possible and looking at the furniture is one of the best ways of seeing if exposed parts are true. However. if a nearby line of a corner or other surface is inaccurate. be careful not to be misled by an optical illustion.

If it is possible to view door openings or frames from an edge. they can be checked for twist. Although plywood can be pulled to conform to slight irregularities. the twist may show on the finished surface. Doors will not conform to a twist, so care is needed to get doorways accurate.

Prefabricating Furniture

When the place where built-in furniture is to be fitted is reasonably true, with vertical, flat walls at right angles, it is usually possible to make furniture in its entirety before bringing it into position. This is not difficult where the furniture is to be hung or fitted to a wall without utilizing a corner, as in a hanging bookcase. Corner items can usually also be prefabricated if walls are vertical and the corner angle can be duplicated. It is furniture to fit in a recess that needs really careful dimensioning.

SHELVING

A simple unit for a recess unit is a block of storage shelves (Fig. 20-1A). The construction depends partly on the decor of the room. All parts could be veneered particle board or blockboard, with joints doweled or screwed (Fig. 20-1B). Front edges should be covered with matching veneer.

For a painted finish there could be a similar construction, but without the veneers. It is possible to sand and fill the exposed edges so paint will cover and finish smoothly, but many coats may be needed. It is better to edge particle board, blockboard, or plywood with a wood strip. A simple glued joint may be adequate (Fig. 20-1C), but a tongue-and-groove joint is

veneer

A

B

C

D

E

Fig. 20-1. Shelving in a recess may be made as a unit, using particle board and plywood, with lipping and edging to give an appearance of solidity on face surfaces.

203

better (Fig. 20-1D). In some situations there may be a metal molding with the nails covered by a plastic insert (Fig. 20-1E).

The unit can be made lighter and cheaper by using thinner plywood or hardboard for some of the panels. If the top is to come above eye level, there can be a rabbeted front (Fig. 20-1F). If the unit is to come lower and the top is to form a working surface, the plywood may be flush on top.

A shelf may be built up in the same way. Ends can also be given a solid look, although actually made with thin panels recessed into rabbets at the back and front (Fig. 20-1G). Screws to the wall then go through the uprights. Where a part is visible on both sides, as may happen with the bottom of the unit, it could be built up with plywood or hardboard on strips, with the front edge rabbeted (Fig. 20-1H). Or the edges could be covered by a strip glued on (Fig. 20-1I).

This type of unit may have its back open so the wall covering shows through. It will then be fixed at the ends. This will generally be adequate, but if the unit is long and may carry much of a load, it is advisable to allow for a few fastenings into the rear wall. There may be metal mirror plates fixed to the backs of shelves or divisions to take screws, but stiffening is added if one or more strips go right across (Fig. 20-1J). The unit may seem stiff enough without back attachments when first fitted, but it could develop a sag after some time in use.

A plywood or hardboard back also helps to keep the unit in shape, and rear mounting screws can be driven through it. A closed back is usually preferable to an open back.

PREFABRICATED CABINET

Another commonly prefabricated construction is a cabinet, usually at table height, which fits into a corner or recess. It could fill an alcove in a living room and be painted to match the decor, or it could be made in a quality wood with a polished finish to match other furniture. It can be an attractive piece of furniture in its own right. In a bathroom or kitchen it may include a sink, and exposed surfaces may be covered in Formica.

Cabinet Measurements

Use a marked rod for making the key measurements. It is usually helpful to make one end piece first, as this will give most of the measurements for other parts. It could be a piece of manufactured board at least ½ in. thick. It could also be framed plywood or hardboard. If it is to come against a wall, the panel may be on the inside of the framing (Fig. 20-2A). An exposed end will have the plywood or hardboard outside (Fig. 20-2B). Glue and pins may be used, and there is really no need to do more than butt the meeting parts together, although halving or tenon joints may be used at the corners if you wish.

In the overall width of the end, allow for the back. This can merely overlap if hidden in the recess. Or it can be covered by a rabbeted edge if the end will be visible. At the front allow for

Fig. 20-2. Built-in storage space is framed so the outside conforms to any irregularities of the walls, but the inside is true and smooth.

the thickness of a doorpost. Prepare the joints for lengthwise parts (Fig. 20-2C). Try the end in position, then make the opposite end to match.

Cabinet Construction

In most cabinets it is best to make any shelves loose so they can be lifted out. Supports are fitted across the ends, and the shelf may be cut around any framing (Fig. 20-3A). For a very long shelf it is advisable to arrange an intermediate support to a post between the doors (Fig. 20-3B) and supplement this with a rail along the back. If there is a post between the doors, check that it will be possible to remove the shelf through a doorway. It may be necessary to halve the shelf, with a joint on the middle support.

At the bottom of the cabinet it is usually best to have a plinth a few inches high and set back a short distance. The base of the cabinet comes above this (Fig. 20-3C). The base may be thick enough to support itself like a shelf, or it may be thinner plywood. In any case it is always well to let an exposed edge have a look of strength. Whatever the thickness of the base, its front may have a rabbeted strip of wood wide enough to come over the plinth (Fig. 20-3D). The ends of the base are supported on strips. The base may extend below the doors, or it can be cut back far enough to be covered by them. The second method needs less careful fitting.

Fig. 20-3. The bottom of the cabinet is raised on a plinth, which can allow for an uneven floor.

206

The number of lengthwise parts depends on the size of the unit, but having a back strip under the top with a greater width than depth allows for screwing from below. At the front it looks better to have a fairly deep strip above the doors. Lengthwise pieces notch into the end framing and may be glued, screwed, or nailed. The back panel should be fitted soon to give the whole structure rigidity, but it is advisable to try the unit in position before this is cut. Then cut and fit the back panel temporarily, and try again before fixing the panel permanently.

The top is best made of a single piece. For kitchen or bathroom it may be Formica-covered particle board. For a living room it may be veneered. For a simple worktop there may be an overlap at the front and at any exposed end (Fig. 20-4 and Fig. 20-5). This may be veneered or covered with Formica, but even ¾ or 1 in. particle board or blockboard looks fragile on the edge, and it is better to thicken it. This should certainly be done for better quality furniture. A Formica or veneered edge can be thickened and all visible surfaces covered (Fig. 20-5B).

Various moldings can be used to build up a front to a better appearance. There may be a simple chamfered piece of wood and a half-round molding above (Fig. 20-5C) or a more elaborate molding can be used, but consider the surroundings and any nearby molded edges. An excessively ornate molding does not look right if the rest of the decor is simple and modern, yet it might fit in well with Victorian furniture.

Cabinet Doors

Doors may be the simple flush paneled types described earlier. If some decoration is required, there may be half-round or other moldings fixed to the surface. If the surroundings are more traditional or colonial, it would be better to have framed doors.

The corners of a traditional framed door are mortise-and-tenon jointed, and a panel either fits into a front rabbet or into grooves. For modern construction, dowels might be used instead of tenons. The simplest construction has the plywood panel between strips of quarter-round molding (Fig. 20-6A).

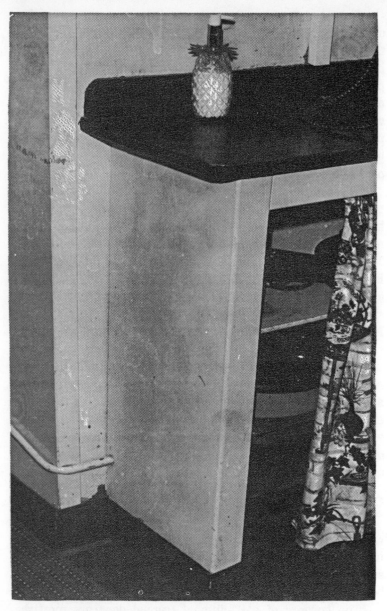

Fig. 20-4. This simple paneled storage unit is open to the floor.

This allows plain joints at the corners, but it is better to rabbet the framing and only have molding at the front (Fig. 20-6B). This is also the method to use for a glass panel.

Fig. 20-5. The cabinet top may overhang and be given a thickened edge.

The strongest paneled door has the panel set into plowed grooves (Fig. 20-6C). The edges of the frames may be molded, or the molding may be fixed after the door is assembled.

Another attractive arrangement is a patterned veneered-plywood panel, used with an attractive wood frame in a natural finish, with the plywood flush in a rabbet and with half-round molding covering the joint (Fig. 20-6D). This method can be used with a painted finish, possible with the panel a different color than the frame. Or the panel might be finished with wall covering.

In this sort of unit it is the front edge of the top and the doors which form the main design features. The front edge normally appears as a sort of wrapover of the top, so it is usual to have this all in the same finish—stained and polished, or painted—but not always in the same finish as the doors and parts visible around them.

Fig. 20-6. Panels may be recessed into frames between separate moldings; there can also be rabbets or grooves.

The doors will have hinges and handles, and in some situations, attractive handles may be all the decoration needed. In other situations the handles may be simple and the beauty of the piece may come from attractively proportioned paneled doors. Usually only the knuckles of hinges show, or they may be completely hidden; but there are decorative hinges intended to be mounted on the surface. If these are used, they should complement the handles.

Using Manufactured Boards

Although most furniture can be made from natural wood—and this is preferable when there is a traditional theme to be maintained—much use can be made of manufactured boards in various forms. Some information on the use of these boards has been given in earlier chapters, and some of the techniques are the same as for solid wood; but since many of the projects in the following chapters can be made with manufactured boards, a summary of special considerations and methods is appropriate here.

SURFACES

Most boards are supplied already surfaced with veneer or a plastic laminate. This is on both broad surfaces and the long edges, but not always at the ends. Unless the base material is very thick and can resist warping from the pull on one side, it is best to have the material veneered on both sides. For economy the veneer on the second side may be of a plain type for locations where the second side is hidden.

BASE MATERIAL

How the board is worked depends mainly on the base material. If it is built up, whether with many laminations of veneer or with a solid core, it can be treated in nearly the same way as solid wood.

The material is more likely to be a particle board in which wood chips and resin are bonded together. Working this material depends to a certain extend on the consistency and proportions. In many cases the amount of wood in the mixture is sufficient for the whole to have characteristics fairly close to those of solid wood. In other cases the mixture may have more tendency to crumble and chip if not worked correctly. If manufactured board of a type you have not previously used has to be cut and a new edge finished, it may be advisable to treat it as this more brittle type at first.

SIZES

One of the advantages of manufactured boards is the availability of stock sizes. But to take advantage of this, furniture has to be designed accordingly. Available sizes must be checked and allowed for early in the planning stage. This has a limiting effect on possible designs, and there is an inevitable slab appearance about many furniture items made from manufactured board. This may be acceptable in a modern decor, but if something different is wanted, the plainness can be broken up by the use of molding, turned parts, and shaped pieces made from solid wood.

Some veneered boards can be matched with solid-wood parts, but boards covered with plastic are not so easily matched, and these are better used with painted parts. Or the plastic-surfaced panel may be separated from the wood parts by a molding or contrasting strip.

CUTTING

Care in cutting is needed if the veneer is not to splinter or break away. It is advisable to cut through the veneer all around with a knife before sawing (Fig. 21-1A), whether cutting is to be by handsaw or power saw. A fine saw is particularly important with a resin-rich particle board.

An ordinary steel saw will do, but if much sawing of manufactured board has to be done, it is better to have a saw with specially tipped teeth that resists blunting.

Crumbling or chipping of an edge is less likely if a handsaw cuts at a fairly flat angle (B) or a circular saw just goes through. Toward the end of a cut, made sure the waste, as well as the main part of the board, is supported, and take the final strokes slowly.

Fig. 21-1. Particle and other manufactured board can be cut with woodworking tools.

EDGING

Plane the edges, if possible, preferably by hand with a tool having a low cutting angle. If you use power planing, pass the material over the cutters slowly; faster progress may cause breaking out. Power sanding is less satisfactory, as this tends to round edges. As a cut edge may have to butt against another piece or be veneered, the surface must be truly flat right to the edges.

The most convenient way to veneer an edge is to use a self-adhesive strip. This ensures a glue that suits the material. If a plain veneer is used, it may be necessary to experiment to find a suitable glue if there are no recommendations with the board or veneer. An impact adhesive is usually satisfactory.

To obtain a good adhesion right to the edge, it is best to have the edge veneer oversize (Fig. 21-2A) so it can be trimmed afterwards. To mimize the risk of an exposed edge lifting, there should be a very slight bevel—perhaps just one stroke of a finely set plane (Fig. 21-2B).

A plastic surface may be cut and treated in a very similar way, but there are special scrapers that will trim an edge better than a plane. A fine file can be used on a beveled edge.

Fig. 21-2. Manufactured board can be covered with a veneer of plastic or wood (A through D); a clearance hole in the board below (E) is needed to take screw shanks.

Manufactured boards may appear flimsy when used over much length, even if they actually have sufficient stiffness. A more substantial appearance can be obtained by using a strip of the same material set back a little below an edge (Fig. 20-2C), or an edge can be thickened so a new veneer or strip of Formica can be put on (Fig. 20-2D). This may be anything from a doubling of the thickness to quite a deep apron on a bar front or similar place.

Reasonable success may be expected from driving ordinary wood screws into manufactured board, but with a particle board, drill sizes should be carefully chosen. Otherwise a screw may shear off before it is fully driven, or there may be breaking out at the surface, or even complete bursting of the board. With most boards a hole should go the full depth of the screw, and if any part of the unthreaded neck will enter the board, there should be a clearance hole to take it

(Fig. 21-2E). In some cases it may be more satisfactory to use a self-tapping screw.

FASTENING MANUFACTURED BOARDS

In some manufactured boards, direct screwing may be satisfactory for attaching fittings or for places where there is only a light load, but at points of greater stress, something else may be preferable. In places where the other side is hidden, a bolt may go right through to a washer and nut.

Dowels make satisfactory joints in most manufactured boards. The dowel diameter should not be much more than one-third the total thickness of a board. In a simple T-joint, use at least three dowels and arrange them about 2 in. apart, with the outer dowels not less than about ¾ in. from the edges to reduce the risk of damage when drilling. Have the work and drill supported in relation to each other to reduce any risk of breaking out.

To strengthen a screwed joint, use a plug in a hole. This may be a piece of dowel glued in (Fig. 21-3A), but it is better to use a plastic insert designed for the purpose. Even when the base material is plywood or blockboard, an insert will make a stronger joint in edge screwing, where the threads would otherwise only come on loose-gripping end grain.

There are plastic joint pieces that can be used in right-angled corners. Two or more should be used, depending

Fig. 21-3. Screws may be driven in to plugs, and special screwed joints can be used.

on the total width. These have an advantage if the parts may have to be dismantled sometime. In one type, there are two plastic blocks that screw to the panels and are joined by a screw (Fig. 21-3B).

DRAWERS

Joints have to be kept simple. It is possible to groove most manufactured boards to take a lip of solid wood, but dovetail and mortise-and-tenon joints are not likely to be successful. This affects drawer construction. Corners may overlap and be glued and screwed, and a false overlapping front used (Fig. 21-4A). The plywood or hardboard bottom also overlaps instead of being slotted in. This means it is better to use slides at the sides (Fig. 21-4B) instead of runners underneath.

It is usually better for drawer construction to be in solid wood. One way of using veneered board for drawer fronts is to make them sloping so the lower edge of a front hides the

Fig. 21-4. Simplified drawer construction.

drawer runners. This provides a lip which can be used for a handle (Fig. 21-4C).

Veneered boards are supplied with true surfaces already sanded. The veneer is quite thin. This means there is little room for heavy sanding, and it is important that the existing surface is not damaged. Vise jaws should be covered with some material which is smooth and no harder than the veneer, perhaps paper or cloth. This is also advisable on the bench top. Plastic-surfaced boards are less susceptible to damage, but if any damage is done, it cannot be repaired. Handle these boards in the same cautious way as veneered boards.

The adhesives used to fix veneers and laminated-plastic surfaces to the core material in manufactured boards are usually highly water-resistant. Some may weaken if exposed to exceptionally moist conditions. Excessive moisture might also affect some core materials. Where a board is veneered all around, it is unlikely that moisture will penetrate enough to have any effect on the core or adhesive except in complete immersion.

When a board has been cut and the edge is exposed some protection against moisture may be advisable. On a cut end that will be joined with dowels to another piece, glue in the joint may be all that is needed to keep out moisture. On an exposed edge, painting or varnishing will probably prevent penetration of moisture. It may be better to first give the edge a coating of waterproof glue, applied like paint, and then sand lightly before painting.

Other liquids may be expected to have the same effect on veneers as they would on solid wood, so the appropriate surface treatment should be used. The plastic used for most laminated surfaces is unaffected by most common liquids, so these surfaces are appropriate for places where food is to be prepared or drinks served.

Room Dividers

Much built-in furniture goes flat against a wall or into a recess. This is a good way of utilizing space, which is often the main reason for building in furniture. An alternative use of built-in furniture comes when a room has to be divided, but without the positive division that would come from the erection of a wall.

A shelved room divider can separate parts of a room used for different purposes: A study area can be kept apart from the more general living area; the area used for eating can be divided from the part used for relaxing. This can be done without making too complete a barrier, particularly if the shelves are arranged to be accessible from both sides. In a large room such an arrangement allows for dual use without people in the two parts being out of touch with each other. The divider could also serve as a display space or breakfast area. It might accommodate books, a radio, a tape recorder, or other items. If the lower part is enclosed with doors, it can be used for storage of things that would not be put on display.

PLANNING

It is not always easy to visualize how a planned divider or projecting block of shelves will look, and sometimes a final assembly of a different size would be better than what is first planned. A shelf a little wider might be better for a record player; a projecting length a little less might make movement less restricted; a working surface might be better higher or lower.

Making a drawing to scale, with a section of the room included, will give some idea of sizes and the appearance and effect of the divider. Where possible, it is helpful to make a mockup. This can be card, boxes, existing furniture, spare strips of wood—anything that can be put in position to indicate size and shape. Manufactured boards are particularly suitable for dividers and shelves, so if the work can be arranged to use stock sizes, the actual construction will be simplified. The convenience of this will have to be balanced against the intended use of the divider and the floor space allocated. Planning is even more important in building something to project into the room than for furniture for against a wall.

CONFIGURATIONS OF DIVIDERS

There are a great many possibilities. The basic divider may be regarded as a block of shelves fixed to the floor and one wall and projecting part way across a room (Fig. 22-1A). This may be entirely open shelving, or the lower part may be enclosed with doors (Fig. 22-1B). The divider may go to the ceiling and be fixed to it, or it may be lower (Fig. 22-1C). It may go only a short way into the room to form a decorative feature without having much dividing effect (Fig. 22-1D), or it may go so far that only a small space is left to pass around the end (Fig. 22-1E). It is possible to let the divider go right across a room and allow a doorway at some intermediate point (Fig. 22-1F). The divider may be cut off at a working height for activities in a children's room or to serve as a bar (Fig. 22-1G). There may be some existing buttress, fireplace, or other projection that can be continued (Fig. 22-1H).

The divider may have shelves open to both sides so things can be reached from either side and people in the two parts of the room can communicate with each other. If more privacy is wanted, shelves can have enclosed backs. The reverse side can have covering to match the room walls and can be decorated with pictures or used as a notice or display board. With wide

Fig. 22-1. Room dividers can be arranged in many ways, from simple projecting shelves to those going the full width and including closed spaces.

shelves, privacy can be provided with dividing panels along the centers of the shelves; then the shelves may be used for different things on opposite sides. This is a particularly useful device for books, as a row of books is not very attractive from behind.

If there are doors over the lower shelves, they can come on one or both sides. If they are on one side, the other side should have a fixed back, which may extend behind the display shelves if privacy is wanted.

Drawers can be included. If a working top is to be used for eating and drinking, there can be a cutlery drawer, which can open from one side in the usual way or can be made to slide to either side. There could be a complete block of drawers working in this way, but there are difficulties in providing stops, so there could be a risk of a drawer being inadvertently pulled completely out. If the divider is being used as a bench for model making or some other activity that requires many tools, drawers are both convenient and tidy.

DESIGNING THE DIVIDER FOR THE ROOM

The design of a divider or block of shelves must be related to the rest of the room and its contents. Consider lighting, both natural and artificial. Electrical lighting can be rearranged if necessary, but natural light from windows cannot usually be altered. If there are two or more windows, an open-shelved divider is unlikely to result in any unacceptably dark areas; but the availability of natural light must be considered, particularly if window area is small or a mostly enclosed divider is planned.

If a divider is to look light, design it so that closed parts are low and the shelf spacing decreases with height (Fig. 22-2A). Having higher shelves shorter also lightens appearance (Fig. 22-2B). Using light-colored wood or paint also helps. If more than one color is involved, the lighter color should be above the other.

If there is to be an effect of solidity or heaviness, possibly in contrast to a very lightly decorated room, there may be high doors (Fig. 22-2C), and upper parts may be longer than lower parts. Fortunately fitness for purpose will usually produce satisfying results esthetically.

Fig. 22-2. Divider design considerations. For a light appearance, decrease shelf spacing with height (A) and make higher shelves shorter (B). For a look of solidity, use high doors and make high parts wider than lower parts (C).

SIMPLE DIVIDER

The construction of a divider with an enclosed lower part and a few shelves is straightforward (Fig. 22-3). Exposed

Fig. 22-3. Room divider construction usually uncludes a raised bottom, an upright against the wall, and intermediate supports. Projecting parts should be rounded.

ends, particularly at the levels where anyone passing might touch them, should be rounded (Fig. 22-4A). This means that if prepared veneered or plastic surfaces boards are used, a matching veneer should be used to cover the shaped ends. Alternatively there might be a molding taken around the end. To maintain the design feature, higher shelves should also be shaped, although if they are set back, they may be cut square across.

The bottom should be raised on a plinth (Fig. 22-4B), or short legs (Fig. 22-4C). The legs should lift the bottom high enough for cleaning beneath. It would probably be advisable to use a matching board up the wall, with shelves doweled or fitted into dado joints (Fig. 22-4D); but each shelf may be bracketed to the wall, particularly if the wall covering seems more effective if carried right through (Fig. 22-4E). In any case the attachment of the shelves at the wall end should be very secure. The base may be screwed to the floor, but if the

Fig. 22-4. Room dividers offer scope for many variations in detail.

top does not go to the ceiling, loads or shocks on most parts of the divider will be transmitted to fastenings at the wall end of the shelving.

In some circumstances there may be a solid upright at the free end of the divider. This makes for rigidity, but it seems more appropriate to library shelving than a room divider. Where the divider is intended to make an almost wall-like division between two areas, a solid end may be appropriate, and it should certainly be used if a door or screen will be attached.

The alternatives at the end are many. There may be pieces of the same section as the shelves, either doweled or dadoed. As it is difficult to get a series of short pieces precisely in line above each other and slight discrepancies will be rather obvious, it is better to stagger positions (Fig. 22-5A). If shelves are more than about 3 ft long, particularly if they are to be heavily loaded, intermediate supports are advisable.

A lighter and more airy effect comes from using pillars. They may be plain round rods, located by holes at their ends (Fig. 22-5B) or taken into metal fittings or turned wood pieces (Fig. 22-5C). If standard pillars are bought, they should be obtained first, as their size may affect shelf spacing. Anyone

224

with a lathe can make his own pillars (Fig. 22-5D), giving a more individual effect to the divider.

It may be possible to use a single fairly substantial post at one side. Then shelves are notches into it and brackets are tenoned in to support the width (Fig. 22-5E). It would be possible to take the post centrally through the shelves. Then the shelves are cut away to pass around it, and supporting pieces are fixed below (Fig. 22-5F). An alternative is to make the post in pieces with interconnected tenons (Fig. 22-5G).

Fig. 22-5. Staggered vertical shelf dividers (A) eliminate the need for accuracy in alignment. The free end of the divider can take many support variations: round rods going into holes (B) or fittings (C); turned pillars (D); a post notched for shelves (E); a post with shelf supports (F); a two-piece post going through the shelves (G); door arrangements (H).

Doors may fit between uprights or overlap them, but the shelf above a door should overhang it. It may be better to have the door above the bottom shelf than to cut the shelf back to allow the door to overlap (Fig. 22-5H). At the wall end the doorpost should be a few inches wide so the door opens well clear of the wall.

BAR WITH DRAWERS

A bar-type divider has a practical use. It allows people on one side to see into the other part of the room, yet it serves as a recognized partition: those preparing food can use the bar as a means of making others keep their distance. As the bar will usually be used with high stools, the height should be decided by experiment, but 36 in. is reasonable.

The top may be covered with Formica and edged with a metal molding. There could be one or two drawers, and the front might slope back to increase foot space (see Fig. 22-5).

Fig. 22-6. A bar is made similarly to a room divider but one side is closed.

As with a divider, the attachment to the wall should be strong. As the back will not normally be visible from the front, it might be solid wood, blockboard, or particle board without veneer. The outer end is also solid, and it may have shelves built on to it (Fig. 22-7A).

Put rails at the bottom drawer level (Fig. 22-7B) and arrange runners and kickers between them (Fig. 22-7C). Make sure opposite sides match and the drawers are at right angles to the sides if they are to be openable from both sides.

Plywood can be used for the sloping front. If there are shelves at the other side and the plywood is fixed to them, this will brace the bar, and the plywood will be adequately stiffened (Fig. 22-7D).

Instead of plywood, the front might be made of hardboard fluted or decorated in some other way. However, hardboard is not as able to stand up to kicks, which it may get accidentally. It is also possible to use wallpaper or upholstering on the front.

If the bar is to be used for hot food or alcoholic drinks, it will need a surface that will resist these things. There are

Fig. 22-7. It is convenient for a bar to have a drawer accessible from both sides, but otherwise construction follows normal practice.

plastic surfaces with wood grain effects that matches the wood in the bar. The edge may be thickened and Formica or other plastic taken around it to show a more substantial edge (Fig. 22-7E).

Drawers have to be made with two fronts. Of course, the fronts cannot overlap, as the drawers are to slide through both ways. Sides can be dovetailed to the fronts or, more simply rabbeted (Fig. 22-8A). A plywood bottom may be slid into grooves before the second side is fitted to the fronts (Fig. 22-8B), or strips may be used inside (Fig. 22-8C). These strips at the sides also increase the bearing area of the drawer on the runners and reduce wear—which may be important if the drawer is expected to get much use. Make sure the bottom edges of the fronts and any strips fixed to them do not project as low as the sides, otherwise they may catch on framing and interfere with the smooth action of the drawer.

Fig. 22-8. Drawer components in the bar may be dovetailed (A) or rabbeted (B); strips inside (C) will help reduce wear. The wall end of the bar can be extended upward to provide decoration or storage space (D).

In some situations the wall end of the bar may be continued upward, even as far as the ceiling. It can then be fitted with shelves or hooks for mugs. It might carry a mirror (Fig. 22-8D) or pictures.

DIVIDER WITH TABLE

A divider may incorporate other things. There can be a flap to swing down to form a writing desk, with compartments for stationery hidden behind it. A cocktail cabinet may be built in. A record or tape deck may be permanently installed, with speakers at the ends of the divider. It is also often useful to let the divider incorporate a piece of occasional furniture that may be brought into use whenever needed. A table-top larger than can be provided by the working surface of the divider itself is an example.

To include a table at a useful height, there has to be a part at about 30 in. above the floor (Fig. 22-9) big enough to provide space for the table. How the rest of the divider is made depends on requirements; it could be made in any of the ways already suggested, but the example shown provides some more ideas.

The main part of the divider is made as already described, with shelves securely fixed into the uprights. It can be treated as a unit, except for the extension of the top. The tabletop is round, with a center part wide enough to overlap the divider shelf sufficiently for the extension pieces to hang down when not required (Fig. 22-10A). Although it could be made from solid wood, it is probably better made of blockboard or particle board with a suitable veneer.

At the center there is a bolt to pass down through the shelf. The bolthead may be recessed into the wood and secured with a plate. The bolthead must be prevented from turning. If it is carefully set into the wood, that may provide sufficient grip, or it can be brazed or welded to the plate. A locknut keeps the bolt from loosening. For smooth action there should be a piece of stout cloth, plastic, or rubber sheeting fixed with adhesive under the tabletop (Fig. 22-10B). This may cover the part of the shelf that will be under the tabletop; or there may be a piece of about 6 in. diameter around the bolt, and strips farther

Fig. 22-9. A room divider can be embellished by turning. This divider includes a round folding table in the unit.

out towards the circumference of the tabletop. Having separate pieces may be advisable if the hinges project at all under the top.

The hinges should be *back flaps*. These will swing back more than normal hinges so the table flaps can hang down (Fig. 22-10C).

Traditional drop-leaf tables have the meeting edges worked with a *rule joint* molding (FIg. 22-10D). (This may be done in solid wood, but manufactured boards cannot be shaped satisfactorily in this way.) If it is done, the total effect is improved if the table edge is also molded (Fig. 22-10E). To bring the table into use, the flaps are lifted and the top turned through a right angle.

Fig. 22-10. Details of the room divider's table top.

In the example the shelf supporting the table has rails underneath and two legs. The legs could be square, preferably with a slight taper, but turned legs complement the round

231

tabletop (Fig. 22-11A). The legs are joined with a lower piece that takes the end of a central rail. This allows more leg room for anyone sitting at the table than if the divider had been continued full width.

What comes above the table depends on the design and size of the divider. If it is not very high, there need be nothing extending from the main block. A shelf extending above the table without plenty of clearance might seem overpowering, but if the total height is perhaps 5 ft. it is possible to let the top extend and have another shelf below it. A pillar to support these shelves should carry through the design of the legs (Fig. 22-11B).

In the example the doors are shown as sliding. They could be plywood or glass, and this is often more convenient than having swinging doors if space near the divider is resticted. However, swinging doors give better access to the interior, as sliding doors never expose more than half the inside.

For sliding doors in anything except the smallest sizes, it is best to buy a suitable door track and guides made of metal

Fig. 22-11. Turned legs complement the round table top; the design can be carried into the shelf
supports (B). Guides that are
screwed in (C) allow easy door removal.

232

or plastic. Such guides give a smoother action than anything that can be made from wood. If guides are made, pieces of hardwood may be grooved and screwed in place (Fig. 22-11C); then if the doors have to be removed, the screws can be withdrawn to release the guides. Door edges, whether wood or glass, should be smooth and their corners rounded. The grooves should be sanded smooth and lubricated either with graphite (the end of a pencil) or candle wax—not oil or grease.

Although our ancestors probably never thought of room dividers, the effect of this piece of furniture with a round tabletop and turned legs and pillar is Jacobean. If this theme is to be carried through to finality, the finish should be brown oak.

CLOSED BACKS

In most pieces of furniture the back is hidden and little care is lavished on its finish. If a divider is to have one side closed, the exposed side of the back paneling is at least as important as the side with shelves and doors. If it is to be hidden by wallpaper, it need not be of select veneer, but it

Fig. 22-12. A rabbeted joint at the top rear edge of the divider hides the plywood (A); the back can be made more attractive with molding (B). A paneled appearance could be obtained by using another molding (C).

should be flat and smooth. Even then, something might have to be done to break up the plainness of the surface.

At the top and wall edges the plywood may merely overlap, but anywhere that this joint would show the edge of the plywood, it would be better to have a rabbet (Fig. 22-12A).

The plainness of the back can be broken up by using moldings. The edge may be covered by molding, using mitered corners (Fig. 22-12B). If the finish is polish or varnish over veneer, a paneled appearance can be obtained by using another light molding (Fig. 22-12C).

Of course, there may be other uses for a plain back. If behind the divider there is a study or working area, the back may have shelves and racks to suit what is being done there. In a bedroom this might be a place to hang clothing.

A divider gives the opportunity for a lot of new thinking about a room, and its design offers plenty of scope for individuality.

Kitchen Furniture

With all of the equipment that goes into a modern kitchen, any built-in furniture has to be planned to fill gaps rather than provide the main furnishing. Fortunately most kitchen equipment is now made to a standard height, which simplifies matching appliances with built-in items. If built-in furniture is to be used in new kitchen, there is more scope for planning than there would be with an existing kitchen.

It is helpful, with a new kitchen, to have a scale drawing of the floor plan, with windows, heaters, and doors marked. Cut out, to scale, card shapes of the things in the room and move these around to try various layouts. Consider heights. Be careful that a high item does not come where it would shield the light from some other item.

Normally the size of the room only allows the fixed items to be placed around the walls, but if there is space, it may be helpful to let a working top or some other floor-standing item project into the room. This may act as a breakfast bar or a room divider.

Before building everything in tightly, consider the ventilation requirements of appliances. Also, there must be space for fresh room air to be admitted and used air exhausted.

The neatest and most practical arrangement is having front edges in line, so it may be necessary to build out anything which is shallow. However, if the kitchen is small and every inch of open floor space is valuable, it may be better to set things back as close to the wall as possible and let the front edges come as they will. The item that projects most should be placed toward the end rather than near the center of a wall so as to be less of a hazard to anyone passing by it. If there is a piece of floor-standing equipment that is only occasionally used, it may be feasible to have it under a fixed top for storage.

If the kitchen can be planned as a whole, it can be given a pleasing appearance by using matching colors, worktop finishes, and handles throughout. With existing equipment installed, some differences may have to be accepted.

The best use of space is usually achieved by having the working surfaces uncluttered and back toward the wall, with enough space above them to admit the usual mixers, pots and pans, and other things used in food preparation. Farther up the wall there can be storage shelves and cupboards. These should have their bases high enough so as not to obscure the view of the working tops, and they should usually not project as far from the wall as the working tops.

After trying layouts with card cutouts on a scale drawing, sketch the arrangements on the walls (Fig. 23-1A). Even better, if you can imagine it, try to depict appearances pictorially (Fig. 23-1B).

The actual construction of built-in items for a kitchen can be much the same as for cabinets already described, but some specific suggestions are given next. Although many items can be made as units—and they may have to be where a stove or other item comes between built-in items—it is always better to carry through such things as the rails under the front of a top to ensure uniformity and stability.

SINK UNIT

The sink unit will usually set the design pattern for other built-ins, so it should be made first. The top will have to be obtained and the woodwork planned to suit it. A common arrangement has drawers and doors below the top. Although

Fig. 23-1. The floor plan shows the arrangement of kitchen units at working level. The pictorial rendition shows the higher storage units as well.

there cannot be a drawer at the sink position, a dummy drawer front may be located there for appearance (Fig. 23-2A). Before the details of construction are planned, the plumbing layout should be settled. By a little readjustment of framing at the back of the unit, the amount of cutting away for pipes may be reduced. The wall may form the back of the unit, which will simplify plumbing; but if the wall is uneven, it is better to have a plywood or hardboard back.

Arrange the bottom of the unit a few inches above the floor to allow for a plinth (Fig. 23-2B). There can be solid wood under the doors, and plywood farther back. Although thinner plywood may be used for divisions and the outside casing, heavy things may be stored under the sink, and it is advisable to use plywood not less than ⅜ in. thick for the bottom.

Doors may ovarlap the sides and either meet at a post or overlap one (Fig. 23-2C). In any case, the post will also take the end of a shelf support. The shelf may come just above half the internal height, and it is usually better to keep it back a few inches from the doors (Fig. 23-2D). If plywood is used, thicken the front and add a support along and under the back.

Fig. 23-2. A basic construction plan for kitchen cabinets. The sink part has a matching front panel (A). Doors may overlap the bottom (B). A central divider also supports a shelf (C and D).

Ends can be plywood or hardboard framed inside. Drawers can be made in any of the ways described earlier. Wood or metal door slides are satisfactory.

How the top is fixed depends on its design. A metal top may come with its edge turned under. This can be allowed to hang over the front, but at the ends and back it is better to either make a rabbet around the top edge of the wood or build up the parts to suit (Fig. 23-3). If screw holes are provided, they can be used; but if the woodwork is made a push fit into the metal edges and some jointing compound or mastic is used to bed the top down, there should be no need for screws.

Fig. 23-3. The metal covering on the worktop overhangs built-up sections at the unit's ends and back.

Complete all internal work before fixing the top, including painting and checking the fit and action of the drawers. Make a trial assembly of the doors, then remove them and their fittings for painting.

KITCHEN STORAGE UNITS

A cabinet can be made in the same way as the sink unit, but with a particle board or blockboard top covered with Formica. This should match the sink unit and other items. If any clampon kitchen device is to be used, make sure that the top is not too thick for the clamps. The top looks better if it is thickened slightly, and this gives a better gluing area for edging strips of Formica (Fig. 23-4A).

If the back of the unit is to be open to the wall, it is usually best to start by making up the front of the unit together with an end. Use a straightedge and spirit level with these parts to define points where the top edge of wall battens should come, then fix these parts to the wall (Fig. 23-4B).

If a washing machine, dryer, or other equipment that has to be moved is to be housed under the working top, the floor will have to be the bottom of the cabinet. Or the unit can have one part with a bottom and another part open to the floor. There may be a door where the movable machine goes, or the front may be left open (Fig. 23-4C).

A working top in a corner is convenient as a working area, but access to all of the space underneath is not always easy to arrange. If a one storage unit comes up to the corner, the other overlaps its end and there is no direct access to the corner (Fig. 23-4D). This is probably the best place to store something that has to pull out. Less frequently used items also can go in the corner and can be reached when the larger equipment is withdrawn.

Fig. 23-4. Details of kitchen storage unit with worktop.

KITCHEN WALL STORAGE

Many kitchen implements can be hung from the wall or put on shelves. To a certain extent, hanging itmes may be regarded as decorative. A rail with a row of hooks is preferable to hooks attached directly to the wall. The top of the rail should slope so it does not collect dust. A piece of veneered or Formica-covered manufactured board, or plain wood finished with gloss paint or varnish, can be used.

Perforated hardboard may be held off the wall with battens so hooks can be put through the holes. This allows a convenient change of layout. Shelves should be given a Formica finish for the sake of appearance and hygiene.

The kitchen looks neater if most things are hidden in drawers or behind doors. There is usually space along the wall, in the angle between wall and ceiling for a cupboard. Cupboard storage can extend from the ceiling down to a point that does not interfere with use of the worktop. It is usually possible to make the bottom shelf reachable from the floor. Doors may swing or slide. but sliding doors are more suitable for long cupboards than for narrow ones (Fig. 23-5A).

Arrange swinging doors so they give the most convenient access. This means an end door swinging toward the wall, but it could also mean the next door swinging the same way if it comes over a working surface in a corner (Fig. 23-5B).

A high cupboard can be simply framed (Fig. 23-5C) and the walls and ceiling used for sides, so not much material is required. However, the strain on fastenings can be considerable when the shelves are fully loaded, so provide plenty of support (Fig. 23-5D).

The doors may be plywood or hardboard on strip wood (Fig. 23-5E). Except for large doors, there should be no need for intermediate strips.

An alternative is to have glass panels. There may be glass sliding doors, or a wood door can be made as a frame to take glass (Fig. 23-5F). In the latter case, use a rabbet and hold the

Fig. 23-5. Overhead storage. Doors have to be designed to give access and not obscure light.

241

glass in with a bead. Then, if the glass has to be replaced, this can be done without damaging the door.

Glass doors allow things to be seen through them and allow light to pass through. In some situations opening a solid door blocks the light from the working area.

COMBINED KITCHEN CABINETS

In a very small kitchen there may be some advantage in letting one unit go from floor to ceiling (Fig. 23-6A). The whole assembly is basically a working top with storage underneath, but with its sides going up to support the upper storage shelves or cupboards. This relieves the wall and ceiling of much of the load and may be advisable if you are doubtful about the holding power of these parts.

There can be narrow shelves at the back (Fig. 23-6B) and there can be hooks for cups inside the uprights. Of course, the working area is limited, but this unit will make the most use of available space.

Fig. 23-6. In a compact kitchen much of the storage can be concentrated in one fitting, which can be cut back if floor space is limited. A flap gives a working surface.

There can be a drop-front working area (Fig. 23-7). This can come as part of a large block of storage space (Fig. 23-8A) or it can be part of a shallower tall cabinet in a very tiny kitchen (Such as the one shown in Fig. 23-6).

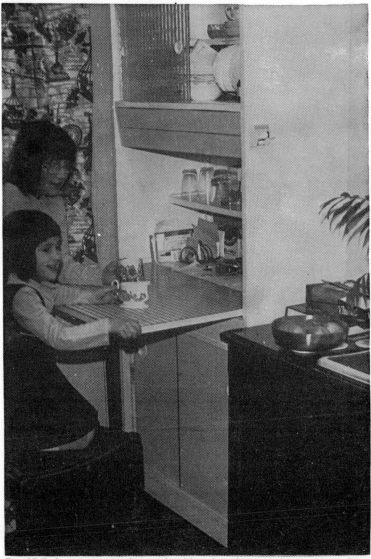

Fig. 23-7. A compact kitchen unit with a drop-front working surface. The lower part has sliding plywood doors, and the upper part has glass doors. In both cases, sunken round handles are used. The drawers under the top part have their fronts extended downward to provide finger grips.

The front could swing down on hinges or one long piano hinge (Fig. 23-8B), or it could pivot on metal rods through the sides (Fig. 23-8C). The front could swing under the shelf (Fig. 23-8D), or it could be flush with the shelf so stops on the

Fig. 23-8. The drop-front working area could be part of a large storage unit (A). It could swing down on hinges (B), pivot on a rod (C), swing under a shelf (D), or it could be supported by stops on uprights (E). Folding stays at the sides give added strength (F).

uprights hold it in the down position (Fig. 23-8E). In a small cabinet the overlap of the flap with the shelf or stops may be stiff enough to withstand working loads on the front, but there could be folding stays at the sides as well (Fig. 23-8F).

244

The lower part of this unit may have open shelves or doors, but in a very confined space the sides may have to be cut back to allow for foot space (Fig. 23-9).

Fig. 23-9. Where floor space is limited, the sides of the unit may have to be cut back.

The hinged flap is best made of particle board with Formica on both sides and preferably around the edges. Ball catches may be used at each side to hold the flap up. The inside of the unit should be painted a light color. The outisde can be painted to match the inside or surrounding colors, but avoid a dark color on a small unit, as this would make it seem even smaller.

There may be spaces to fill between the sides of kitchen equipment. These may be only a few inches wide, but they should be closed to give a uniform appearance around the walls. Filler pieces can be made which match the built-in furniture and merely press into place so it is easy to remove them if an appliance has to be withdrawn for servicing.

Space Savers

24

Built-in items can be useful and helpful and decorative in confined spaces. These items also provide an opportunity of using up leftovers from larger projects.

These smaller items may come flat against a wall or may be worked into a corner beside a door. They can occupy a small recess or other place too narrow for a free-standing piece of furniture. If they are fixed to the wall and do not reach the floor, they do not restrict walking space. In general, the attraction of small built-in items is in utilizing small spaces.

The design of space-economizing built-in furniture is very dependent on actual situations, so many variations are possible. The amount of projection from a wall may be governed by the distance from the wall to the edge of a doorway in a corner. The location of a mirror may be determined by the available light and how far it is possible to stand from the mirror in a narrow passage. Any shelving may have to suit particular items that will stand on it. Some suggestions are given next that can be adapted to suit these and other circumstances.

HALL MIRRORS

A mirror near an outside door allows anyone passing in or out to make a quick check on his appearance. It should make some provision for hair and clothes brushes and might include coat hooks.

Mirrors with Shelves

A simple mirror with a shelf is shown in Fig. 24-1A. The exposed edges are cut with curves, which give a more graceful effect than straight lines. As the mirror determines the sizes of other parts, this should be obtained first. Suggested sizes are given. It is possible to frame the top of the mirror. Otherwise the exposed mirror edges should be ground and polished.

The sides (Fig. 24-1B) are cut with two rabbets—one for the mirror and one for the backing plywood. This makes it possible to fix the assembly to the wall without the glass, using screws through the plywood, and then slide the mirror in from the top. If there is not enough clearance to do this, the mirror may be inserted before fixing to the wall and some brass mirror plates used at the sides. The glass makes the unit quite heavy for its size. There should be two or more stout screws fairly high and one or more farther down.

Fig. 24-1. In narrow passageways, mirrors and shelves can be fixed to the wall without restricting floor space.

248

The shelf can be fitted into a dado joint at each end (Fig. 24-1C). Dowels can also be used, and a simple template (Fig. 24-1D) can be used to make the holes.

A filler piece (Fig. 24-1E) goes below the mirror and shelf. The plywood backing can be cut to match the top of the mirror or can be taken straight across between the sides (Fig. 24-1F). Check that the rabbets for the glass will allow it to slide in easily yet be free from wobble after it is inserted. Then stain and varnish the woodwork. If there is any risk of dampness, a coat of varnish on the back of the mirror itself will reduce the risk of damage to the silvering by moisture.

A variation on this (Fig. 24-2A) has hooks for brushes. It can be made in the same way as the first mirror, with extra backing at one side. The simple design shown gets its beauty from the grain of the wood rather than shaping of the sides.

The basic part is the plywood back, whose shape is determined by the size of the mirror (Fig. 24-2B). The shelf is thickened at the back for stiffness. Tapering from below avoids a heavy look (Fig. 24-2C). The strip for the brush hooks has a rabbet to suit the glass (Fig. 24-2D). A lip on its edge covers the plywood and provides a support for the top (Fig. 24-2E). At the opposite side a rabbeted strip projects the same amount (Fig. 24-2F). The single rabbet is sufficiently deep for the glass as well as the plywood. The top is a strip of wood which fits over side strips and the back after the glass has been fitted (Fig. 24-2G). Mounting is done with screws through the plywood. If there is insufficient space above to slide the mirror in after the woodwork has been fixed to the wall, the assembly can be made to swing if one of the upper screws is through the side wood. The screw which will come behind the glass is driven, then the assembly is swung on this to allow the glass to be fitted (Fig. 24-3). Then the unit is positioned and the other screw is driven.

Mirror With Clothes Hooks

Clothes hooks may be mounted on wings extending from each side of the mirror frame (Fig. 24-4A). The mirror is fully framed, and it can be held in place with a plywood back and fastenings in the same way as a picture is framed (Fig. 24-4B).

Fig. 24-2. One variation of the mirror has hooks for brushes (A). The back conforms to mirror size (B) and the shelf is tapered to avoid a heavy look (C). The rabbeted strip for brush hooks (D) has a lip that conceals the plywood (E). Final framing includes installing the other side and top (F and G).

24"

24"

3"

pivot on screw

Fig. 24-3. If there is not enough clearance above the unit to allow sliding the mirror in from the top, the unit can be mounted so it pivots to allow the mirror to be installed from the side.

The woodwork can be doweled together. The traditional method would be to use mortise-and-tenon joints (Fig. 24-4C), but it is possible to halve some parts and supplement glue with screws driven from the back (Fig.24-4D). Edges may be finished by working a mold around the outline if a power molding tool is available.

Coat hooks may be bought or wooden pegs turned on a lathe (Fig. 24-4E). Pieces of dowel could be inserted in holes at an angle. If the holes cannot be made on a drilling machine with a tilting table, the holes can be made at a uniform angle by drilling freehand through a block of wood with a suitable hole (Fig. 24-4F).

Fig. 24-4. A hall mirror can be extended to provide clothes-hanging space.

SHELVING

Shelves can be arranged to make use of space that would otherwise serve no purpose. A block of shelves may go along a wall from the corner by a door (Fig. 24-5 and 24-6A). The

Fig. 24-5. A bookcase designed to fit the corner space between a door and radiator. Note that the plinth is set back and painted black; the end up-right is kept back from the heat of the radiator.

number of shelves and their size will depend on the situation, but a width to suit books is suitable for a living room.

In the design shown, construction can be made with dado joints or dowels. If the uprights are narrower than the shelves

(Fig. 24-6B), intermediate dado joints may go right through. Joints are stopped elsewhere (Fig. 24-6C). Having the piece at the door end narrower facilitates fitting against molding (Fig. 24-6D) and allows shelves a little wider than they might otherwise.

In most places a plinth under the bottom shelf (Fig. 24-6E) is advisable, and there may be a plywood back with a covering strip above the top shelf (Fig. 24-6F) to protect the wall from articles on the shelf.

Fig. 24-6. The corner next to a doorway may take a bookshelf.

A similar arrangement can be used for the storage of cleaning tools (fig. 24-7A). Hooks for hanging smaller brushes and other tools can be driven into uprights and other members. At the bottom there can be a rail to keep bottles and cans in place (Fig. 24-7B).

Another convenient place for a shelf is above a radiator. There should be a gap of several inches to keep the shelf from becoming too hot.

253

The simplest shelf is a piece of wood on brackets (Fig. 24-7C). Wooden brackets look better than ordinary metal shelf brackets. End brackets may be extended as shown to keep from sliding off the ends (Fig. 24-7D). One end can extend into a block of shelves (Fig. 24-7E). Such a unit might be used below one of the mirrors already described. The single shelf could continue up into a block of shelves.

Fig. 24-7. Other storage units can be made like the bookshelf shown in the previous illustration.

The shelf over a radiator could be extended for the telephone and its accessories. The telephone part will have to be at least 5 in. wide. It can be built out with a piece glued on and possibly strengthened with dowels (Fig. 24-8A). The most compact arrangement has the telephone parallel with the wall, but if the extra projection will not matter, putting the telephone on an angle produces an interesting appearance (Fig. 24-8B). To prevent the instrument from being knocked off the shelf, there can be holes to take its feet or strips or wood to form a frame around it.

One way of accommodating the directory and other papers is to make an open-sided compartment into which they can slide from the side, beneath the telephone shelf (Fig. 24-8C).

Another way is to make a box compartment that will tilt forward yet hide its contents when closed (Fig. 24-8D). A hanger is fixed to the wall and may hide one or more metal shelf brackets. The box is lightly made of plywood and may have its front framed to improve appearance. There are two hinges at the bottom of the back, and a chain limits swing. One or a pair of ball catches at the top will hold the box in the closed position.

Fig. 24-8. A shelf may be broadened to take a telephone (A) and have a bin below it for a directory (B through D).

WALL DRESSING TABLE

In the smallest bedrooms or those already full of furniture, the only way to fit in a dressing table is to keep it as shallow as possible and suspend it from the wall. The accompanying mirror is fixed to the wall above the table and not attached to the table.

In one version (Fig. 24-9A), the top, which may be veneered or plastic-covered plywood or particle board, is bracketed to the wall and given legs which taper back to provide minimum floor obstruction. There may be shelf as well. If there is a plywood back between the top and the shelf, this may be stiffened to take fastenings to the wall.

Doweled construction is best for particle board. With solid wood you might use a dovetail dado joint between uprights and top (Fig. 24-9B), which will prevent warping. A simpler alternative is to use screwed and glued blocks on one or both sides of the uprights (Fig. 24-9C).

Front edges could be molded or beveled. With this and other shelf assemblies at about waist level, it is always advisable to round projecting corners to minimize damage to the structure and any person bumping it.

Fig. 24-9. In a small bedroom a dressing table can be arranged below a wall mirror. The table is supported so there is little obstruction at floor level.

A Lighter Dressing Table

If the theme of the room is more open and light, a more delicately framed structure is preferable. This can be achieved by using rods or legs instead of solid uprights. A plain top can be bracketed to the wall and given a drawer or shelf and round legs (Fig. 24-10A). There may be more legs and more shelves, or a broad shelf may take the place of the drawer.

The top may be bracketed, as in the other type, or there can be a backboard fixed to the wall and a batten below (Fig. 24-10B). Screws are driven from the batten into the top (Fig.

24-10C). As the legs will take much of the downward load, possible strain on wall fastenings is not as great.

The backs of shelves can also rest on battens (Fig. 24-10D). The legs may be the prepared type with ferrules and end fittings. In that case their length may determine the height of the top. Alternatively, use dowel rods of about 1 in. diameter or make suitable legs on a lathe. At the legs will take much of the downward load, possible strain on wall fastenings is not as great.

The backs of lower shelves can also rest on battens (Fig. 24-10D). The legs may be prepared type with ferrules and end fittings. In that case their length may determine the height of the top. Alternatively, use dowel rods of about 1 in. diameter or make suitable legs on a lathe. At the lower shelf level the leg goes straight through. A peg, preferably metal, goes through the leg to support the shelf, and a washer goes above that (Fig. 24-10E).

The drawer can have rabbeted lap joints (Fig. 24-10F). The bottom may be glued and nailed from below or recessed into grooves. If the drawer is set under the top and the facing extends below the front, there will be no need for a handle (Fig. 24-10G). The simplest way of hanging the drawer is to put runners along the top edges and make supports for these under the top (Fig. 24-10H).

BATHROOM FITTING

Although a bathroom is occupied only briefly, there are many toilet articles to be accommodated in a small room, and keeping all these things tidy means having quite compact fittings. A suggested bathroom fixture is shown in Fig. 24-11A.

Because of the damp atmosphere, the wood needs protecting. This can be done with suitable paint. Plastic-covered manufactured board may also be used, providing it has waterproof glue holding the plastic laminations. It is also possible to use glass instead of wood for some shelves. This gives a hygienic appearance, as does a finish in a light pastel shade.

Although the fitting may have to be supported mainly by the wall, stronger support is obtained if it is possible to take

Fig. 24-10. Construction details for a lighter dressing table.

one or more parts to the floor. If one end is in a corner, additional fastenings can go through the end to provide more strength. It is advisable to avoid plain iron or steel fastenings because of rust.

Construction is by any of the usual methods. The mirror may be framed, or it could be fixed with domed-head screws through holes in the glass. The best place for a strip light is over the mirror. Glass shelves can rest on wooden brackets, preferably with front lips to keep the glass from sliding in (Fig. 24-11B). Metal fittings for glass shelves can be used. Some of these allow for adjustment to different heights, which may be an advantage if the storage arrangements are changed.

There are always a great many things in a bathroom which are better hidden, so a door is advisable over part of the

Fig. 24-11. In a small bathroom a mirror and storage fixture can be hung from the wall. A leg to the floor can give additional support.

fixture. (Fig. 24-11C). If this is kept tall and narrow, a stock size of particle board may be used, hiding whatever number of shelves are required.

Other items may be hung outside the fixture, either with hooks or brackets, and towel rails may be slung underneath.

Fireside Fittings

25

A living room benefits from having a focal point. In the days when the only means of heating was solid fuel burned in an open fire, the fireplace was the focal point. Modern central heating is very attractice, but it does not provide a focal point. Because of this, some homes still have a fireplace, even if for practical purposes it may be unnecessary.

A wall-mounted electric heater or a gas fire may also serve as a focal point. The electric heater may also produce a simulated log or coal fire that creates the right look even when heat is not needed. Such a unit's purpose as a focal point can be enhanced by building a furniture unit around it. The room is then planned so seating and activities in the room will be directed towards the wall with the heater. Anything built in should provide storage as well as decoration complementary to the use of the room. The design may vary from something compact, arranged in the immediate vicinity of the heater, to a complex fitting that covers the whole of a wall.

The built-in unit will usually be designed to suit the size of the heating unit. It may also be necessary to take into account access for maintenance. Cables, switches, and pipes should not be covered if they may have to be reached later. A small unit can be fixed to the wall with a few screws so it can be removed quickly if the heater has to be serviced. Access for servicing a larger unit while it is in position may need to be considered.

So that air can circulate around the heater, all woodwork should be kept away from it. How far depends on the particular unit. but 3 in. at the sides and 6 in. at the top are probable minimums. If the fitting projects far in front of the heater, any woodwork above may have to be cut back to allow hot air to rise and prevent the wood from getting too hot. Heating efficiency will be improved and the wood protected from overheating if a piece of metal, curved to throw the rising hot air forward. is mounted below the shelf and over the heater.

Whether to have a projection at floor level is a matter of personal preference. This dates from the days when burning coal or wood might fall out of the fire; a hearth was provided to catch it. Besides giving the traditional effect, a hearth prevents the unit from being kicked and helps to keep persons from getting too close to the heat source.

SIMPLE FIRE SURROUND

In this unit (Fig. 25-1). a mantel shelf joins two blocks of shelves at the sides, which may be used for books or

Fig. 25-1. The days of the fireplace and open fire may have passed, but an electric heater with storage shelves around it can provide a focal point in a room.

ornaments. The heater is measured and sufficient clearance allowed. The top should usually be at least 30 in. from the floor, even if this gives a very wide gap above the heater. There may be space for another shelf below the top. The shelf depth depends on the purpose and situation. About 5 in. is necessary for most books. As little as 3 in. may be right for ornaments, particularly in a small room, where too much projection might look overpowering.

Make a dimensioned sketch or a drawing showing the main lines to scale to see if proportions look right and to decide on the sizes of wood needed. If manufactured board is used, it may be possible to design the unit to use stock sizes and avoid waste and unnecessary cuts.

If there is a base molding around the room, it may be possible to cut it away. If not, the fitting must be cut around it. The edge of the plywood above the molding should be prevented from warping by applying a piece of half-round or other molding (Fig. 25-2A).

Allow for a strip across the top (Fig. 25-2B) to support and stiffen the top. Rising hot air may cause light-sectioned solid wood to warp, so it is advisable to use not less than 1 in. thickness and to include a front stiffener if the central gap is more than about 2 ft. (Fig. 25-2C). Manufactured board should not warp. Solid wood will not warp if a piece is chosen with the annual rings going across the thickness (Fig. 25-3D).

If solid wood and traditional methods are preferred, preparation for the back is made by rabbeting the parts where it will fit. The rear piece under the top may be rabbeted for the full length if this is easier, as the central rabbet is unlikely to show. Top corners can be dovetailed (Fig. 25-2E) with the inner uprights in dado joints and the rear strip passing through (Fig. 25-2F). Shelves are also fitted into dado grooves (Fig. 25-2G). The outer uprights can go into dovetail or rabbet joints (Fig. 25-2H).

In a simpler construction the joints are made with screwed blocks, which can be bought as plastic units or made from strip wood (Fig. 25-3A). The success of this construciton depends on accurate cutting of ends. Neatness at the top corners is achieved if the top overlaps (Fig. 25-3B). Bottoms may be

Fig. 25-2. The fire surround can be made with traditional joints in wood.

screwed into uprights. If the top is to be veneered, screws may be driven through the top into the uprights. Counterbored holes and plugs are used with the screws.

If there is to be a base under the heater, this could be plywood covered with Formica. It should be fixed, but for convenience in cleaning, it should be removable. It can be

Fig. 25-3. If the surround is made of a manufactured board, simpler joints can be used.

made narrow enough to fit between the shelf units, or it can be cut back to butt against them (Fig. 25-3C). A similar idea can be used if the base is to run the full width of the unit, letting the wood sides of the base butt against the outer uprights.

LARGER SURROUND

The basic design can be extended outward and upward. The result may be an assembly of cupboards, shelves, and racks over an entire wall. Although such a design may be thought of as one unit, it is usually best to divide it into parts which are assembled separately and brought together. In this way, satisfactory construction is easier, and there is less risk of parts being out of square. With a single assembly involving many compartments, some part will not come to a right angle whatever is done—probably due to an accumulation of small errors leading up to that point. This can be minimized if independent modules are made.

Although a large surround may consist entirely of shelves, it is usually better for convenience and appearance to provide doors so some of the shelves become closets. There may be a second shelf on top (Fig. 25-4).

Construction is generally similar to that of the simpler unit described earlier. In a traditional construction, the lower top may use a combination dado-and-dovetail joint (Fig. 25-5A). In the simpler construction, blocks below the shelf may be sufficient, although a dado adds strength (Fig. 25-5B). The lower top piece should be cut back over the heater to the same width as the upper piece (Fig. 25-5C).

If hinged doors are used, they may be placed between the uprights (Fig. 25-6A) or may overlap them (Fig. 25-6B). In any case, the shelf above the door should overlap it to keep out dust.

Small sliding doors may be glass or plywood in grooves. The grooves are best made by strips of wood glued in place. If the top groove is made deep enough, the door can be lifted out (Fig. 25-6C). For larger wooden doors it is advisable to use a sliding doortrack, as wood sliding on wood can offer too much resistance. Get the sliding-door fittings before settling the final

Fig.25-4. The fire surround can be elaborated to have doors and extra shelving.

Fig. 25-5. Dovetail joints interlock the main parts of the larger surround.

sizes of the design, as it may be possible to modify the design slightly to suit the fittings.

With doors that reach to the bottom, the hearthlike bottom should have a flush top (Fig. 25-6D). A raised edge would necessitate having the door bottom high enough to swing over it. The bottom can be made with plywood supported by framing, using a strip under the closet fronts and sufficient cross members for stiffness (Fig. 25-6E).

Of course, this unit is susceptible to many modifications. It need not be symmetrical. It may have a much larger extension on one side than the other. The purpose of each part may be adapted to match other furniture. If one side is near a sewing machine, that side can be entirely closed with doors for storage of sewing equipment; the other side may consist entirely of book shelves. There could be sliding doors at one side, hinged doors at the other side. The sliding doors could come above open shelves instead of below, especially if they are glass doors covering displayed items.

FOLDING SEAT

A heater surround can incorporate a pair of folding stools that close into the unit and can be drawn out for use. Comfort

Fig. 25-6. Some of the shelves in the surround can be made into closets by closing them with doors, which may hinge or silde.

controls sizes. In use the top should be 12 to 15 in,. above the floor. so the hinge line should be at this height (Fig. 25-7A). It is possible to have the seat fold down, but it is easier to have it fold up. There must be enough height above the hinge line to allow for this, the height being the depth of the seat. For an overall height of 30 in., this is 15 in. (Fig. 25-7B). Although a wide seat may be most comfortable, having the width and height about the same allows the stool to fold inconspicuously (Fig. 25-7C).

The top of the stool and the front support can both be made of veneered manufactured board, or they can be blockboard with solid wood lipping glued on. The hinges should be substantial as they and their screws tave to take the weight of a sitting person. Similarly, the shelf to which the stool is attached must be strong and securely jointed to the uprights at its ends.

There are ways of relieving the hinges of some of the load. A piece below the shelf edge will take the rear edge of the seat when down (Fig. 25-7D). And if the front support is set back

Fig. 25-7. Another elaboration for a fire surround is a pair of seats that fold up when not in use.

from the edge of the top (Fig. 25-7E), its edge can rest against the top in the down position and take part of the thrust. In the folded position this leaves a gap at the top, however.

A folding strut should be fitted to hold the front support of the seat upright and prevent unintentional closing. A ball catch holds the assembly up when folded.

Living Room Furniture

26

In rooms used during the day, there is a case for a combination of built-in and free-standing furniture. There is usually an accumulation of books, games, radio and television sets, and items for display. One use for built-in furniture is to provide storage for all these things and keep the room tidy.

In most rooms of reasonable size, chairs and tables are more convenient if movable. In a very small room it may be desirable to have a table that folds up to the wall, possibly with bench seats that fold with it. This might be appropriate in a dual-purpose room where a clear floor is desirable at times.

An office or study area is needed in any home. How elaborate this is depends on the work contemplated. If the home is large enough to devote a room to this purpose, it can be equipped as an efficient office; but in most homes a part of a living room has to be used, and some sort of a built-in is the best way of taking care of this requirement.

Furniture should be planned to match the decor of the room. There is a modern trend towards the severely plain. A purely functional unit that is little more than a block of shelves will fit into this sort of scheme. If other furniture in the room is traditional, antique or colonial, some concession to this should be given in planning the built-in furniture. It may be possible to give the appearance of something from a bygone day by adding shaped or fretted pieces or including turned or carved parts. Merely applying pieces that break up the severe outlines may be enough (Fig. 26-1A).

Much of the rather severe built-in furniture lends itself to construction in veneered manufactured boards. The attractive grain of the veneer breaks up the severity of the design. This is particularly so if panels are included which show their surface to the front. Veneered boards may form doors, drop fronts, or forward- and end-facing panels (Fig. 26-1B).

Shelves and other parts that only show their edges may be made of blockboard or particle board without veneer and may be finished by painting. Even if there is no other paintwork on furniture in the room, a neutral or pastel shade will blend into most schemes (Fig. 26-1C).

Fig. 26-1. Valuable storage space can be provided by a large wall unit, which can be given an ornate or severely plain finish to match other furniture.

WALL UNITS

Combined units that cover most of one wall are useful for multipurpose built-in furniture. Total needs should be assessed. Several different layouts may be possible. Using solid wood available in sufficient lengths it may be simplest to carry horizontal lines right through (Fig. 26-2A).

Manufactured board is not usually available in lengths greater than 8 ft. This is usually more than enough for heights, but may not be enough to follow through the whole width. If this material is used, it is better to carry vertical lines through (Fig. 26-2B).

Careful work will let lines in the opposite directon of the followed-through lines match, but the risk of slight discrepancies showing can be reduced if different sections are staggered (Fig. 26-2C).

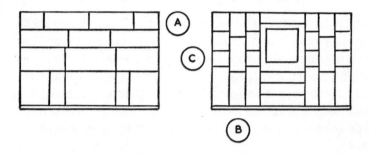

Fig. 26-2. For convenience in construction a large wall unit should be given shelves going right through, or uprights going right through, but not both.

Usually wall units project uniformly from the wall. This simplifies construction, as all parts are the same width. Breaking up the front line however, may improve appearance as well as provide better storage. For instance, a sewing machine may need more back-to-front space than other things, so a section of the wall unit may be made wider (Fig. 26-3A). This may also apply if a drop-front desk is built-in or a chair out of use is to be pushed under a desk (Fig. 26-3B). Alternatively, it may be better to reduce the width in cramped quarters where chairs have to be pushed under (Fig. 26-3C).

If horizontal lines are to follow through, the first parts made should be the shelves, base, and anything else that runs the full length. Mark these together so distances match. The only place where there may be slight deviations is in an end

Fig. 26-3. Side units can be connected by shelves.

which comes against a wall at a corner. Check the wall with a level or plumb line. If it is out of vertical, allow for this in making the end parts. Elsewhere in the unit, upright parts should be truly vertical, and not parallel with a faulty wall. Adjust the ends of horizontal parts accordingly. In an old house with very inaccurate walls, it may be neatest to recess a piece at the front to give a truly vertical start to the new work (Fig. 26-4A).

With the followed-through lines vertical, the method of construction will depend on the overall width. If this is little more than the height, the whole thing can be prefabricated, and there should be no difficulty in erecting and attaching the entire assembly satisfactorily. If there is a large expanse of wall to be covered, it may be better to work in sections. Each section may then be treated separately (Fig. 26-4B). This does mean duplication of some uprights where the sections come together. Actually this double thickness may aid the appearance by emphasizing solidity. There could be a molding over the joint, or just a strip with rounded eges (Fig. 26-4C).

Another way of prefabricating, but without the duplication, is to make up alternate sections and add what comes between after these are in position (Fig. 26-4D). In this case, it is best for the more complicated parts to be in the prefabricated sections.

Much of the construction will be the same as described elsewhere, using dado, doweled, or manufactured joints for the main assembly. For shelves the joints can be permanent, and this helps in stiffening the whole unit; but there are places such as booksehves where height adjustments may be desirable. There can be metal strips which recess into the uprights and allow supports to be located in several places. Alternatively, there can be hooks on metal dowels that fit into holes in the wood or into plastic sockets (Fig. 26-4E). These may also be used for glass shelves, which then can be taken out for cleaning.

Fig. 26-4. If a wall unit fits into a corner, it may be necessary to cover inequalities there (A). Subunits may be made and brought together (B through D). Shelves may be made adjustable with special hooks (E).

The front view is a multiplicity of crossing lines. This may be attractive, but if the line effect is to be reduced, doors and flaps can overlap the framework (Fig. 26-5A). This also applies to drawers (Fig. 26-5B). the fronts hiding the runners.

If a cocktail or drink cabinet is included, this can be lined with Formica and given glass shelves. Doors can accommodate glasses, either standing in racks or hung by their stems (Fig. 26-5C). The door may pivot centrally so everything housed there is brought to the front on semicircular racks (Fig. 26-5D).

Fig. 26-5. The severity of a wall unit can be broken up by drawers, doors, and special storages.

DESKS AND STUDY CORNERS

The essential part of a desk is the worktop. Care is needed in planning to see that this is big enough. Even if it is big enough, it can become cluttered and effectively reduced in size if adequate storage space for other things is not provided. Take into account the many things that will be associated with writing or typing. There is much to be said for building an L-shaped working top into a corner. The typewriter comes around the corner, ready for typing yet out of the way of other desk work (Fig. 26-6A).

The working surface may be permanently in place, possibly with shelves or drawers underneath as in many office desks, but fixed to a wall. It may be given an interesting appearance by sloping it back and using a leg (Fig. 26-6B). Above the working surface there may be an independent wall unit (Fig. 26-6C).

The various things that accumulate on a desk may not be considered to add to the beauty of a room, so a flap front that closed over them may be desirable. This can be arranged in one of the ways described for kitchen cabinet fronts.

Sometimes it is better to have a front that folds downwards. This can be arranged in a simple shallow desk with bookshelves (Fig. 26-6D). The flap can have two or more hinges or a full-length piano hinge. There can be brackets

Fig. 26-6. The needs of a study or desk can be met by a built-in fitting. How elaborate it is depends on requirements.

hinged below (Fig. 26-7A), or there can be a pair of frame legs something like those on a gate leg table (Fig. 26-7B). The legs can be tenoned for maximum rigidity, which may be an advantage if the desk is used for work requiring steadiness.

Fig. 26-7. The flap on a shallow desk with bookshelves can come down to rest on hinged brackets (A), or on hinged frame legs (B).

It is always convenient to have enough space at the back of the working surface for essentials. Things required close at hand, but not quite so often needed, should be given other accommodations. Bookshelves are nearly always needed. A drawer under the fixed top is valuable, but it has to be shallow to allow for a comfortable surface height and knee room below (Fig. 26-8A).

Even when the desk does no more than provide space for dealing with household business, files are desirable. These can

Fig. 26-8. To allow knee room, the drawer under a fixed top has to be shallow (A). The need for a workable home office unit might call for extensive construction (B).

278

go in a deep drawer. A home office unit may develop into a fairly extensive piece of furniture (Fig. 26-8B). If the desk is to form part of a living room, it can be given a good finish and space can be allowed for things like displayed china, picture frames, and mirrors, which will soften for formal business look.

A compact desk designed to rest against an open wall repeats the angle of the sloping front in the legs (Fig. 26-9A). The shelves reach the wall, but the feet are away from it. The flap can be supported by simple hinges with folding stays (Fig. 26-9B). Decorative veneering on the exposed front of the flap will enhance appearance.

Fig. 26-9. A simple flap-type desk with built-in stationery storage need take up little room.

DESK CONSTRUCTION

Construction of the desks described can be done in the ways already described. There can be internal fittings to take papers, envelopes, and all the other paraphenalia that goes with office work. There is satisfaction in making these parts by traditional methods. This involves working with fairly thin wood, which can be joined in several ways. Although the racks and pigeon holes could be built in, they might be made as a unit to lift out (Fig. 26-10A).

If wood of sufficient width and no more than ⅜ in. thickness can be obtained, the corners can be dovetails (Fig.

26-10B). If plywood is used, comb joints may be better (Fig. 26-10C). Divisions can have dado joints. If divisions are to be adjustable, a large number of dado grooves are made so shelves can slide out and be changed (Fig. 26-10D). If the whole construction is to be fixed and all parts are thin, there will be less weakening if V notches (Fig. 26-10E) are used instead of dadoes. All front edges should be rounded, and there may be hollows cut for ease of gripping papers (Fig. 26-10F).

Fig. 26-10. Construction details for a desk.

CORNER FIXTURES

A corner is a good place for displaying china or trophies, so a glass-fronted cabinet is appropriate. The lower part may have a wooden door (Fig. 26-11A).

Although a traditional corner cupboard of this type would have been made of solid wood, this is probably best made today with manufactured board with veneered faces and lipped edges of matching wood (Fig. 26-11B). This piece is shown with a step between the two levels, which necessitates a special joint in the lipping if exposed end grain is to be avoided (Fig. 26-11C).

With the two main parts lipped along their exposed edges, they are joined in the angle, and the other parts are made to fit between them. If the corner of the room is less than a right angle and the cupboard is made a right angle, the front will fit closely and the gap at the back will not show. If the corner is wider than a right angle, a gap at the front will show. Put the main parts in position and temporarily fasten them, then check the angle that will have to be used for the parts between them.

Fig. 26-11. The corner of a room is often wasted; a display cupboard there is attractive and useful.

Wings extend from the main parts, and the doors hang on these. Shelves inside may reach the wings but should be cut back to give clearance to the doors (Fig. 26-12A). If glass shelves are used in the upper part they can rest on narrow battens or hooked studs (Fig. 26-12B). The glass-paneled doors should have tenoned joints to resist any tendency to flex and possibly break the glass. The glass is held by a rabbet with beads (Fig. 26-12C)

Fig. 26-12. Shelves within the display cupboard have to be cut back to clear the doors (A). If they can rest on batten (B). Tenoned joints in the doors (C) resist flexing.

If the usual manufactured board about ⅝ in. thick is used, the door framing should be about 1⅞ by ⅞ in., and the wings should be this size or slightly thicker to give stiffness where they support the door hinges.

It is sometimes possible to extend a corner cabinet along one or both walls. The capacity of a corner cupboard with short wings is slight, but this increases as the wings become wider (or deeper). The door size is reduced, however. If there are extensions, it is reasonable to enlarge the wings until they and the door are about the same width (Fig. 26-13A).

How the extensions are arranged depends on the room and the purpose. Such an assembly can often be made to accommodate a record player and its speakers. It can also serve as a sideboard or bookcase. If there are things to display, some of the doors may be sliding glass. A possible layout is shown in (Fig. 26-13B). Although there could be the usual plinth, this example is shown on short legs.

This sort of built-in furniture can be prefabricated in units—the corner and two separate extensions, or the corner

Fig. 26-13. In a corner assembly, access to the corner has to be considered, the feet have to be high enough for cleaning, and a member to tie parts together should be included.

as part of one side and the other extension separate (Fig. 26-14A). In any case, the top is best treated as a whole, to be applied after the lower parts are fixed. The meeting parts of units can be faced with hardboard or plywood, providing front edges will be covered so as to hide this. A point to watch with a corner door and extensions is that there must be sufficient clearance for the door to swing back without fouling. It is advisable to set back the extension on the hinge side slightly (Fig. 26-14B).

With this sort of assembly it is always good practice to arrange some of the structural parts to tie the assembly together. In the case of an extension-and-corner assembly, a front rail can either be recessed and screwed in place, or it can be dovetailed at its end. Double tenons can come at intermediate vertical parts. The strength can be carried around the corner with a bridle joint (Fig. 26-14C).

FOLDING TABLE

A built-in fixture can include a combination of table and benches sufficiently large to be used for meals. The space behind the folded parts can serve for storage of plates, cups, cutlery, and other things needed for the meal.

The method of folding and supporting the table and seats can be very similar to that shown for stools beside a fire (Fig.

Fig. 26-14. In this example the glass-fronted case is built as a separate unit.

25-7). Arranging parts so some weight is taken off the hinges is important, particularly for a heavy table or a seat for two or three.

The parts fold into a wall unit that is generally similar to one designed for books. The actual size of the table is governed by the height of the room. It will be used at about 30 in. from the floor, and its top cannot be so long as to hit the ceiling when folded (Fig. 26-15A). The bench seats will be hinged lower, so they could be longer; but there is little advantage in them more than a few inches longer than the table (Fig. 26-15B). Getting the lengths in relation to the height of the room should be the first step in planning one of these units. Of course, additional wall width can be used for more storage space.

If the legs must be as close to the tops as possible when folded and there is no room for anything except the hinges, then there could be bolts into the floor to secure the legs in the down position (Fig. 26-15C). If a little more thickness when folded is acceptable, the benches and table may have narrow

Fig. 26-15. A complete dining unit of table and benches can be made to fold into a wall fitting that stores cutlery and dishes.

side pieces and folding metal struts of a type that lock in the down position (Fig. 26-15D).

There may be some advantage in tying the bench and table legs together when down, using a removable crossbar (Fig. 26-16A). This does not prevent accidental folding, but it links the three legs so they resist folding together. A removable strut can also be used diagonally between the top and the leg. It can have a tenon at one end, but the other end will need a locating block and some sort of catch or a turnbutton (Fig. 26-16B).

The table, when folded up, needs a secure fastening. Bolts can be used, although fairly large wooden turnbuttons held by bolts are effective even if not beautiful (Fig. 26-16C). Making them lopsided and loose on their bolts will ensure their dropping to the locked position by gravity.

Fig. 26-16. Joining the table and bench legs with a crossbar keeps them from folding together (A). The table top, held by a strut to the leg when down (B), can be held up when not in use by a turnbuttons (C).

Bedroom Furniture

27

Bedrooms are often smaller than living rooms. Consequently there is less space for free-standing furniture in many bedrooms and more reason for building in. Storage space may be increased by changing from free-standing furniture to built-in furniture. Convenience will also be increased. Some ideas on layout are given in Chapter 1.

It is advisable to have an overall plan before rushing into the making of one item of furniture. It is possible to make one unit that combines dressing table, clothes closet, washing facilities, and maybe a bookcase and other storage. In a very small room the one built-in item and the bed may be all that can be accommodated, but if there is more space, it may be more convenient and attractive if built-in items are divided around the available space instead of being concentrated on one wall.

Consider the position of the door and window. A door may have to swing into the room. If the built-in furniture is to come near the door, it is a good rule to ensure that at any angle of opening the space between the door and furniture is not less than the width of the doorway (Fig. 27-1A).

At a window any new piece of furniture that projects far from the wall for much height should be considered in relation to its blockage of natural light. If the window does not already admit more than enough light, avoid tall, solid blocks of furniture close to the window (Fig. 27-1B).

In a very small room, wall-mounted items that do not reach the floor may add storage capacity or convenience without reducing walking space significantly. It may be possible to arrange for movable furniture like chairs or small tables to be kept under the higher fixed furniture (Fig. 27-1C). It is even possible to provide storage space above head height (Fig. 37-1D).

Fig. 27-1. Plan built-in furniture so door clearance is not reduced (A), light is not obscured (B), clearance for other furniture is not restricted (C), and the built-in unit is out of the way (D).

CORNER DRESSING TABLE

In small bedrooms consider the use of corners. In some arrangements there may be a little waste space in the point of the triangle, but this will be compensated for in convenience. A dressing-table mirror may come across the corner (Fig. 27-2). It need not necessarily be at 45° (Fig. 27-3A). If it is arranged at another angle, there may be some advantage in the use of limited light or space.

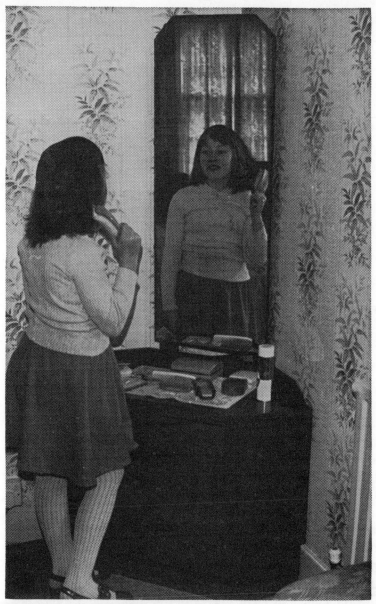

Fig. 27-2. A corner dressing table closely fitted to the walls, with the mirror on uprights against the walls.

If a corner is used, a limitation of drawer shape and capacity has to be accepted. The dresser can have a front with the corners at right angles to the walls, then drawers can be taken as deep as the shape will allow (Fig. 27-3B), narrow drawers going deeper than wide ones. If the corner is other than a right angle, the possible depth of a drawer becomes less, although this can be increased if the back of the drawer is cut on a slant (Fig. 27-3C).

Check the angle of the room corner and make either the actual top or a template to match. It is unwise to assume that the corner is truly a right angle.

Fig. 27-3. A corner dressing table need not make a 45° angle with the walls (A). Drawers have to be arranged to make best use of the unusual geometry involved (B and C).

If the dresser is to be removable, it may be given a plywood back. Otherwise there need only be sufficient framing to support drawer guides and take screws that fasten into the wall. If there is a base molding in the room, this can be cut back, or the dressing table can be cut to fit over it (Fig. 27-4A). It may be possible to have the plinth at the same height as the base molding. It can follow the shape of the front or can be taken straight across (Fig. 27-4B).

The angular vertical joints at the fronts can be mitered and glued. Blocks can be glued in the angles, but if the joints are accurately cut and fitted, sufficient stiffening will probably be given by drawer rails and other framing carried across these angles (Fig. 27-4C). Be careful to make the drawer guides at right angles to the front. The drawers are made in the usual way and may be fitted between the framing or arranged with overlapping fronts.

If maximum capacity is wanted, it may be better to use doors instead of drawers. Whether to have one or two doors depends on the situation. The doors will swing back to the wall, and it is possible to fit racks or shelves inside to take toilet items, cosmetics, etc. (Fig. 27-4D).

If maximum capacity is not of prime importance, one can arrange curved shelf blocks on the doors (Fig. 27-4E). Transparent plastic sheets bent around the curved shelves will keep stored things in place yet allow them to be seen when needed.

A mirror in a corner cannot be arranged to tilt, so the common swinging arrangement cannot be used. This means that the mirror should be fairly tall to suit users of various heights and allow a full-length view. Its lower edge may rest on the top surround (Fig. 27-4F). The mirror is clipped to a piece of plywood screwed to uprights, which are carried down the carcass to provide stiffness (Fig. 27-4G).

Fig. 27-4. Making furniture to fit a corner brings some special problems, but this dressing table takes up minimum space. It may given drawers or doors.

Because its triangular shape makes work on the table more difficult than with a rectangular piece of furniture, it is advisable to construct the table in its entirety before finally fixing it to the wall. There may have to be several trial fittings as work progresses. Complete all but the painting or polishing before screwing the dressing table in place.

BOOKCASE HEADBOARD

A bookcase fitting can be made to go over one or a pair of beds, with one or more shelves. There can be a built-in electric light over a single bed (Fig. 27-5A). Individual lights can be built in over twin beds and the fitting can be brought down between the beds to provide a table (Fig. 27-5B). The bookcase

Fig. 27-5. A bookcase makes a good headboard fitting. It may be cut back to take a reading lamp or extend to the floor between two beds.

need not project more than about 5 in. and will not interfere with movement in the room (Fig. 27-6).

If the fitting is made from solid wood, corners may be dovetailed, rabbeted, or doweled (Fig. 27-7A). Shelves may be extended to allow for dado joints (Fig. 27-7B). There could be an open back so the wall covering shows through, but it is probably better to use a plywood or hardboard back recessed into rabbets (fig. 27-7C).

The light fixture may come under the straight bottom shelf. but it and your head are protected from knocks if the central part of the shelf is raised a few inches (Fig. 27-7D). Books are fairly heavy, so attachment to the wall should be

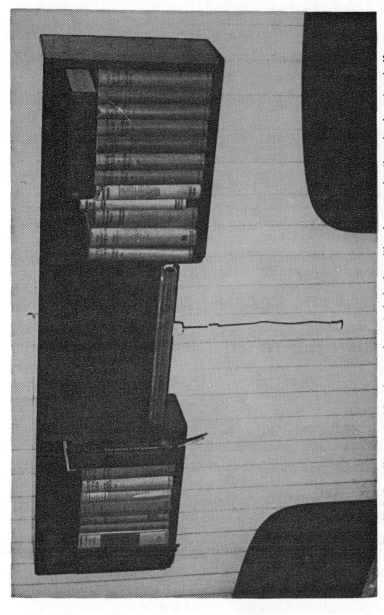

Fig. 27-6. A wall-mounted bookcase above twin beds, with a lamp under the raised center shelf.

strong. The load is best taken by screws to the wall near the top, with a few fastenings lower to keep the bookcase close to the wall. A strip across the back and under the top can take the load-bearing screws, or drilled metal plates can be arranged below the top. If the back is thin plywood or hardboard, screwing directly through that without something to transfer the strain to structural parts may not be sufficient.

Fig. 27-7. The corners of the headboard fitting may be dovetailed, rabbeted, or doweled (A). Shelves can be made to allow for dado joints (B). The hardboard back is recessed into rabbets (C), and the central shelf is raised to accomodate a light fixture below (D).

CHILD'S BOOKCASE HEADBOARD

In a child's bedroom there is a need for a place where drawings, cutouts, and pinups can be temporarily fixed. A child may not have many books to house, so the headboard bookcase can be adapted to provide a pinboard, a display shelf, and limited book space (Fig. 27-8A).

Construction can be with manufactured board or solid wood. A piece of plywood might do for the pinboard, but pins are easier to push into soft boards made for the purpose. There can be a different material behind a shelf (Fig. 27-8B). This need not be the full thickness of the pinboard if it is built up at the lower edge (Fig. 27-8C).

Fig. 27-8. This headboard fitting for a child's bedroom includes a pinboard and mirror.

Fig. 27-9. High cupboards should be made to take loads from the top (A and B). The highest wall fastenings take most of the strain (C). Lifting doors give convenient access (D).

If the unit is more than about 3 ft. long, one or more dividers (Fig. 27-8D), should be fitted to prevent warping of the shelves and help support books . There can be storage shelves on each side of the pinboard, or there can be a mirror at one end (Fig. 27-8E).

High Storage

If there is enough head room to allow a cabinet at ceiling height, construction is straightforward. Remember that loads will come on the unsupported bottom, so plan your work accordingly. If the length can be arranged so the assembly fits in a recess, both ends can be attached to the walls, and most of the load will be taken there. If one end can come in a corner, that end should be firmly attached to the wall. Elsewhere, arrange structural parts to resist pulling apart and to transfer the load to the wall or ceiling. Metal or wooden shelf brackets can be put below to supplement the fastenings through the back.

Vertical members should overlap horizontal members if nails, screws, or dowels are used for joints (Fig. 27-9A). These joints resist side thrusts better than they resist pulling apart. The strongest joints are made with dovetails with the tails in the upright parts and the pins in the horizontal parts (Fig. 27-9B). Covering the structure with plywood, fixed with glue and pins, helps to consolidate the structure and resist any tendency for parts to sag or break away (Fig. 27-9C).

The strongest attachments can be made high at the back. Next strongest are those at the ceiling, then lower fastenings.

How the doors are arranged depends on the use and position of the fitting. The may be hinged vertically, but they will probably require handles fairly low so they can be reached from the floor. Sliding doors can be used if there is little room for swinging doors. In some circumstances it may be better for the doors to swing upwards (Fig. 27-9D). A turnbutton on the ceiling can hold a door up.

More Bedroom Furniture

28

A proposed piece of built-in furniture has to be considered in relation to its ability to serve the uses intended. Functionalism can be checked by regarding the piece as a number of separate units. Hanging space in a clothes closet can be determined by measuring clothes on hangers. Drawer sizes can be determined by measuring what is to go into them. If washing facilities are to be included, stock sizes of tops and washbowls will give you unalterable dimensions to which adjoining parts have to be adjusted.

MULTIPLE UNIT

A great variety of multipurpose built-ins can be made by combining various units with different purposes. For instance, two clothes closets can be made, then a dressing table can be made as a shelf between them (Fig. 28-1A). Each closet may have a swinging door with a mirror inside (Fig. 28-1B). The whole width of the inside may be hanging space, with a shelf above and one or more drawers below (Fig. 28-1C). Drawers that come inside a door do not have space for a handle unless it is a folding one, but notching the drawer front provides a grip without projection (Fig. 28-2).

If the closet is wide, the inside may be divided so there is a block of shelves or small drawers at one side. Wide fronts can

Fig. 28-1. A multipurpose bedroom built-in can be made up of several separate units according to an overall plan. Two clothes closets, for example, can have a dressing table between them (A); each could have a swinging door backed by a mirror (B). Options for the inside include a shelf and drawer (C).

have double doors, which are more convenient and project less when open. Sliding doors do not expose all the contents as swinging doors do, but they may have to be used where there is little space for swinging doors.

In a floor-to-ceiling arrangement in a room with a high ceiling, doors for the full height may be excessively tall. It is then convenient to have a cupboard above the clothes closet (Fig. 28-3). The cupboard can be built into the same structure or it may be a separate unit. It could go across two closets (Fig. 28-4A). The doors should not be too wide, and the handles should be within reach.

In a small fitting the dressing table may be a single piece of veneered manufactured board, but this will gain in appearance and stiffness if there are pieces beneath the back and front (Fig. 28-4B). The front stiffener can be shaped to provide a knee hole (Fig. 28-4C). Alternatively, there may be one or a pair of shallow drawers (Fig. 28-4D) or be curved, swinging compartments for cosmetics (Fig. 28-4E). With a wide dressing-table top, there could be a block of drawers to the floor at one or both sides (Fig. 28-4F).

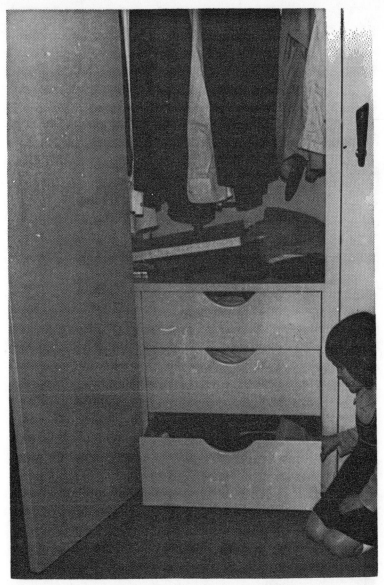

Fig. 28-2. Drawers inside a clothes closet are notched instead of fitted with handles. This way they can be brought farther forward without touching the door when it is closed.

Embellishments

Such a combined unit will look rather plain at this stage. The appearance can be improved without additional

Fig. 28-3. Storage cupboards above the clothes-hanging space give maximum storage space.

construction by using contrasting colors. The drawers, doors, and tabletop could show the wood grain, and the trim and paneling could be painted.

Plainness can be broken up by several other devices. Large decorative handles may be used in a matching system

Fig. 28-4. Cupboards could traverse two closets (A). The dressing table in a small fitting will look better and be sturdier with stiffeners beneath the front and back (B); the one in front could have a knee hole (C). An alternate treatment would be to include drawers (D through F).

for drawers and doors. This can be carried further by having a pair of lamps inside the clothes closets and over the dressing table (Fig. 28-5A), preferably in a style that complements the handles. Another way is to apply moldings to the door fronts (Fig. 28-5B). The moldings could be painted to contrast with the doors; gold on a cream background would give a luxurious appearance.

Fig. 28-5. Decorative touches for a bedroom unit.

A dressing-table mirror can be arranged in several ways. A square or shaped one may be fixed to the wall (Fig. 28-6A). It should be tall enough for people of various heights, either sitting or standing. A mirror may also be supported on adjustable fittings between two pillars on the dressing table, sufficiently far from the wall to allow adequate movement (Fig. 28-6B). The fittings could be on brackets projecting from the wall. A long mirror could have its fittings on the clothes closet sides (Fig. 28-6C).

The space between the clothes closets can be decorated by a cornice (Fig. 28-6D). It may have some sort of decoration, such as a carving. It may hide a fluorescent lamp. There could be drapes hanging from the cornice to the mirror (Fig. 28-6E). Drapes can be very effective in breaking up plainness and integrating the new piece of furniture into the room, particularly if they match other hangings or bed coverings. The drapes could be arranged to draw to the sides and show a mirror or picture.

Sliding Doors

A fitting in which sliding doors are appropriate and often essential, is a bedroom storage unit that runs the full width of

Fig. 28-6. If mirrors are included, they must have room to swing or must be arranged at a height to suit various users. The space over a mirror and dressing table can be decorated with drapes and a cornice.

one wall. This combines clothes closets. chests of drawers, hat shelves. and other storage units. all hidden behind doors. The number of doors depends on the overall width, but these should be about the same widths as the subunits enclosed. With two rails it is then possible to slide doors far enough to completely expose at least one subunit. With the inside divided into fourths and with four doors on two rails. it is possible to expose half the contents at a time.

For this sort of thing it is usually a good idea to make the interior as units. dividing the width of wall into convenient sizes. To avoid duplicating adjoining sides, alternate units can be completely prefabricated and positioned, then the intervening units can be fitted between them.

It is possible to mount the sliding doors on the front of the fitted units. but it may be more convenient to keep the doors and their rails separate. mounting them under a wooden batten across the ceiling a short distance in front of the units.

SMALLER CLOSET

Clothes closets are necessarily large to serve their purpose. For two people the best arrangement usually is two closets arranged as just described. If there is only one person's clothing to be accommodated, a more compact unit is possible. If space is limited, the whole thing can fit into a recess (Fig. 28-7A). Against a straight wall the clothes closet can be arranged in the corner, where its size will be less obtrusive (Fig. 28-7B). The dressing-table top may extended into a bookcase (Fig. 28-7C).

Fig. 28-7. Though clothes storage may take up the most room in a bedroom, other things can be built onto the closet to increase its usefullness and break up its boxlike severity.

Where a table-top comes against a wall, something should be done to prevent damage to the wall covering. A strip of wood on edge may be all that is required (Fig. 28-7D) or there may be a higher piece carrying a shelf (Fig. 28-7E). Where the working area has a washbowl set in, the top and any protection behind it may be plastic, and this can extend a short distance down the front.

Construction Details

Any of the methods described earlier in the book may be used. Veneered manufactured board can be used, but for large areas it can be expensive. An alternative is to build up a framework for the major units, with members at places where shelves and drawers will come, then cover the framework with plywood or hardboard. Pairs of end frames can be made up complete and joined with other parts (Fig. 28-8A). The covering may overlap at corners (Fig. 28-8B). Mitering there for the length of a joint may result in slight discrepancies that will be more apparent than the narrow overlap. Corners can be covered with molding (Fig. 28-8C). Backs and tops may be hardboard or plywood if the wall surface itself is unsuitable at the back of a closet. Any storage place for clothing should be dustproof, so a back as part of the furniture is desirable.

Various types of rails to take clothes hangers can be bought. Quite a simple rail is a dowel or metal tube with its ends in blocks (Fig. 28-8D). If the rail may have to be removed, one end may be in a U-shaped socket instead of a plain hole.

A block of small drawers or trays will accommodate small dress items and jewelry. It is possible to use plastic or metal trays intended for office filing. Similar trays can be made from wood. They can fit close like ordinary drawers, but it is

Fig. 28-8. Simple rods take clothes hangers, ties, and towels. Shoes can go on shelves or a pair of rods, small items in sliding trays, and ties on staggered rods.

convenient to provide them with runners and allow spaces between them (Fig. 28-8E).

Ties, belts, ribbons, and similar items may be better hung on a rail, which could be inside a door. This could be a wooden or metal rod between supports (Fig. 28-8F) or staggered rods projecting from a central support (Fig. 28-8G).

Shoes and other footwear may go at the bottom of a clothes closet or in a shoe cupboard on the end. If there is sufficient depth for suitable shelves, the shoes may lie flat. This arrangement will take the greatest number of shoes in a particular area, but it means a shelf width of at least 12 in. If this much cannot be allowed there may be sloping shelves with ledges to hold the shoes (Fig. 28-8H). This arrangement has the heels downwards. Shoes will take up slightly less space if arranged the other way, either with the shelf cut back to allow heels to hook over the edge or with a pair of dowel rods (Fig. 28-8I).

Shop Equipment

Shop built-in units are generally more utilitarian than those for other parts of the home, so they may be made from wood of lesser quality and sometimes from material left over from other projects. However, anyone who considers himself a craftsman will not be satisfied with crude construction on a fixture that will be in front of his eyes every time he sets about making something in the shop.

Besides correct construction in built-in shop fixtures, an adequate finish is desirable. Too often the wood is left untreated. It gets dirty, harbors dust, and soon looks to be of poorer quality than it is. Varnish is probably the best finish for tool racks and similar things. A light color may be used inside a storage cabinet or other enclosed place to help give maximum visibility in what might be a shaded area.

In a storage space it may be appropriate to do something to indicate where things belong so this can be seen when the tools or other articles are removed. There could be just an outline in a contrasting color, or the shape could be painted in solidly. Red is usual for this sort of thing, as it is the most vivid color. A quick glance at racks for any red showing will show what has not been put back. If others share the tools you use, marking places is a good idea.

CONVERTIBLE WORK AREA

Making large items of furniture or tackling metalworking projects that require heat or machinery may not be appropriate to a living room, but for light wood-work—particularly such things as carving, whittling, and marquetry—a convertible bench might be set up in a living room without causing too much disruption of the main function of the room. The same sort of equipment would also be suitable for other fairly compact and clean hobbies, such as model making, preparing and mounting semiprecious stones, bookbinding, picture framing, and many fabric crafts.

It may be possible to include some power tools, but anything that produces much waste or throws dust into the air is obviously inappropriate. There could be an electric drill with some attachments, but power planers, sanders, lathes, and saws could not be used, except in the smallest sizes, and then a craftsman would usually prefer hand methods.

The prime consideration in planning a workbench that is to convert to something else is whether it has to stand up to wracking strains or not. If wood is to be sawed, planed, or chiseled, or if metal is to sawed, filed, or bent, the whole structure needs to be substantial and firmly braced.

For lighter crafts one of the designs suggested for built-in desks may be suitable, possibly with the worktop made thicker and the stationery racks and drawers replaced by storage for tools and materials. If a flap is to hide all this, its exposed surface may be suitably finished to match other things in the room. A drop flap may not be stiff enough in itself as a worktop except for light activities like dressmaking, although gate leg supports could be made substantial enough to give a reasonably stiff bench top.

It may be better to let the flap swing down to make the fixed top more accessible, but it then covers drawers, shelves, or cupboards that will almost certainly be used for tools or materials. A still better way is to make the flap removable. This allows it to be taken away so there is no risk of it becoming marked during a working period. Its inside may also serve as a drawing board, which will be useful for displaying drawings of the work in hand as well as for making drawings in advance.

A fairly stout worktop should be built with enough overlap on its supports at the front to allow for a clampon vise and other tools (Fig. 29-1). A liftoff flap may overlap the bench to hide it as the bench will almost certainly show signs of wear after a short time. There could be blocks at the bench ends and shaped pieces on the flap to hook over them (Fig. 29-1B) if the working area is enclosed by ends. Otherwise bent metal pieces on the flap could go into slots in the bench (Fig. 29-1C). This method ensures nothing projecting above the working surface when the flap is removed. The top of the flap can be held by catches in the same way as a hinged desk flap.

Fig. 29-1. A bench can be built into a living room piece like a desk, with a liftoff front that hides the worktop. The location of the bench will determine its capacity for overhanging work.

Layouts For Benches

For heavier work the bench needs to be more rigid and firmly braced. If it can come in the angle of a room, fastenings to two walls will provide rigidity, but there are problems. If wood is to be planed, it is usual to have the vise towards the left end of the bench and to plane from right to left. If this action is towards a corner, work capacity is limited (Fig. 29-2A). Placing the bench in the righthand corner is better (Fig. 29-2B). A bench in the center of a wall gives more freedom for long work (Fig. 29-2C), but it needs more internal bracing. A recess gives the best all-round bracing, but for planing, the front of the bench should protrude (Fig. 29-2D).

Fig. 29-2. Placed in a lefthand corner, a bench would restrict planing movement (A); located in a righthand corner (B), the bench offers more freedom of movement. Against the center of a wall, a bench would not be adequately braced. If it is in a recess, make the front protrude (D).

Construction Details

Although a desk could be stiffened to allow for heavy work, it is probably better to make what is really a stout shop-type bench, suitably disguised in its lower parts to look like room furniture, with a top to close over it. The top can be fitted with tool racks and can swing up to have everything ready for work with the minimum preparation (Fig. 29-3).

If the legs are made of furniture wood and if any visible ends, drawer fronts, and doors are made of matching wood or veneered manufactured board, these things and the cover can be given an attractive finish to suit the decor of the room. Alternatively, if a cheaper wood is used, a painted finish may be appropriate. The worktop must be thick enough for its purpose—at least 1½ in. for joinery and cabinetwork—and this can be hidden by the overlap of the top (Fig. 29-4A).

strut

Fig. 29-3. A substantial bench can be built with a lid that takes tools. The lower part can be disguised with drawers and doors if the unit must look like ordinary furniture.

An apron board plays a large part in resisting the loads that come with planing and other work, so it should be included. As it is unlikely that a fixed vise can be used, a flush-front apron cannot be used unless it is cut away for the clamp of a removable vise. It will be better to let the top overhang back inside the legs to give front clearance (Fig. 29-4B). Drawers or doors below the top may be flush with the apron or brought forward (Fig. 29-4C).

The top may be made of particle board. With tools attached it will be quite heavy. The back piece on which it pivots should be fairly stout and firmly attached to the wall. Hinges should be strong enough to take the load, and screws should be long enough so as not to work loose.

How the top is held up depends on the situation. Fastening to the wall is most secure, but this means a fitting on the wall that may not be appropriate in a living room (Fig. 29-4D). If the bench is in a corner, however, the fastening may not be very obtrusive. The alternative is a strut or bracket on the bench (See Fig. 29-3).

SHOP PLANNING

If there is ample space in a shop, a free-standing bench of adequate size and substantial construction has the attraction of allowing movement all around and space for large work to overhang in any direction. A bench braced to the wall gains in rigidity, but there is not the same room for overhang. In a

Fig. 29-4. Construction details for a desklike bench.

small shop a bench as large as possible, braced to wall and floor, is usually a good choice.

If the working surfaces of other fixtures in the shop are the same height as the bench, they can help support things like 8 by 4 ft sheets of plywood. Long work can be more easily dealt with if there are places all around the shop at the same level. The settled height has to suit working with hand tools, which means about 30 in. If the height of a saw bench, combination woodworker, or something else that cannot be changed is already within an inch or so of this, its height might be adopted as the standard height throughout the shop.

In places around the shop not already being used for some other purpose, there can be blocks of shelves or drawers, with tops substantial enough to be used as benches (Fig. 29-5A). If a top is wide enough, it may support something like a tool grinder or drill stand, but make sure there is enough clearance around for anything you expect to work on.

Higher parts of the walls will be mostly used for tool racks and storage. Any units that project far from the wall should be upwards of 18 in. above the worktop level (Fig. 29-5B). This allows the majority of things being worked on to be moved around freely.

STORAGE

It is helpful to store material so it can be seen, yet an abundance of short pieces and offcuts would take up too much

Fig. 29-5. Other substantial bench tops at the same level as the working bench are always handy for supporting work. Storage racks can come against walls.

room if spread out, so there has to be a compromise. Small pieces may have to go on shelves under a bench. Slightly longer pieces are more easily selected if stood on end in a rack (Fig. 29-6A). Have several divisions so that when the rack is not full the remaining pieces do not fall over. The divisions also allow different woods or sizes to be kept apart.

Wood in bulk is quite heavy. Any wall storage racks should have uprights to which the horizontal parts may be securely bracketed. Plywood checks make strong shelf brackets (Fig. 29-5B). It is good practice to make them so the initial angle is a few degrees higher than a right angle, then the inevitable slight sag does not leave the pieces sloping forward. In most shops wood racks of this sort should be open to the sides as well as the ends, but if there is plenty of space, there can be uprights at the front and the wood can be removed endways. Supports should not be more than about 3 ft apart for the sections of wood likely to be stored.

If wood turning is anticipated, a rack for suitable wood may come above the lathe. It can be mounted against the wall and hung from the roof (Fig. 29-7). A few battens can form the

Fig. 29-6. Wood storage ideas for the workshop. Long pieces can stand on end for easy selection (A). Plywood checks (B) help wall brackets take the load of wood bought in bulk.

bearing surfaces, but support them with appropriate joints (Fig. 29-8A)—not nails, which may pull out.

The roof area is often neglected as storage space. So long as anything put there is above head height, an arrangement of hanging racks (Fig. 29-8B) will keep material out of the way and free lower space for more useful purposes. These racks should not interfere with lighting. A point to note is that the roof or ceiling area will be the hottest part of the shop. This means that wood will get warm and dry out. This may be a good thing with some woods and will not matter with most manufactured boards, but some woods need a certain minimum moisture content if they are to remain flat and be easily worked.

TOOL RACKS

Tools may be roughly divided into those that are in fairly constant use and those that aren't. There is no sharp dividing line, and there will be some tools used frequently on one job and not at all on another. Common tools like hammers, mallets, chisels, benchsaws, and ordinary planes should be readily accessible. More specialized planes, carving tools, special screwdrivers, uncommon drills, and other seldom-used tools can be put away where they are protected from rust.

A confirmed craftsman does not buy one tool kit and keep it for the rest of his life. He is likely to make or buy new tools and discard others. Consequently it is unwise to settle on a system of tool storage that may suit what you have now but makes no provision for changes.

Fig. 29-7. A roof rack for wood used for turning is fixed above a rack for turning tools. All are convenient to the lathe. Note the C-clamps hung on a rail below a shelf and the marking gauges at the left in a notched rack.

Fig. 29-8. Battens used to support a shelf for wood used in turning should be secured to uprights with joints.

There is no need for elaborate storage. If a tool will hang on a nail, that may well be the best way to store it, although it may be better to use a dowel projecting from a block. Constant use of a nail may scratch the inside of a grip like a saw handle and make it uncomfortable to hold.

The best position for tools most frequently used is at about eye level, and there can be a strip of wood at this position, extending as far as convenient. Dowels can go into at a slight upward angle (Fig. 29-9A) for hanging tools. Screwdrivers, spikes, awls, and similar items can fit through holes a plywood strip (Fig. 29-9B). Other tools may be better entered into slots from the front, preferably with the plywood given a slight upward slope (Fig. 29-9C).

Fig. 29-9. Storage for tools give plenty of use for built-in racks, some of which can be quite simple.

Edged tools should not be hung so their cutting edges are exposed. Chisels and gouges may go through slots in a rack with a piece of trasparent plastic in front (Fig. 29-10 and

318

Fig. 29-10. A rack for chisels and gouges, with the blades protected by a piece of transparent plastic.

29-11A). Planes may go in a rack with their edges towards the wooden back (Fig. 29-11B). As this projects forward a few inches, the ends can have racks for other small tools (Fig. 29-11C).

Another line of racks may go higher for tools that are often used, but not quite as frequently as those below. C-clamps can go on a rail. Long tools like pump-action screwdrivers and bar clamps will have to be hung higher to allow for their length (Fig. 29-11D). In some cases, smaller tools may go between them.

In a much-used shop, open racks as just described are the best way of storing the common tools, but if there are intervals when the shop is out of use or if children also use the room, it may be better to have the tool racks behind doors. The insides of the doors can be used for racks, but the cabinet must be planned to allow for the thickness of tools on the doors plus the greatest thickness of a tool inside. The insides of the doors are probably best kept for thin items, such as sheets of abrasive, rules, and flat tools (Fig. 29-11E).

The inside of a tool cabinet must be readily accessible. This rules out sliding doors. If hinges doors are used, there

Fig. 29-11. Specilaized storage for particular tools: a rack closed with plastic for chisels and gouges (A); a rack that protects the edge of planes (B) and includes an extension for small tools (C); a high rack for long tools (D); a rack within a door for flat items (E).

must be room for them to swing back without interfering with tools on the walls. It may be better to use liftoff panels instead of doors or to have the doors swing up (Fig. 29-12A).

If space were unlimited, the drawers might be divided so every tool would have its allotted place. Unfortunately, too many compartments of this sort reduce capacity considerably, the racks taking up more room than the tools they hold. Consequently. tool storage in drawers has to be a compromise between just throwing tools in together and giving each a special place.

Carving tools need separate storage so their edges do not get damaged. They may go in a compartmented roll or be recessed in a board (Fig. 29-12B). Wood-boring bits may also

Fig. 29-12. A swing-up door gives easy access to a tool cabinet (A). Carving tools need the protection of tailored storage (B). A compartmented drawer (C) holds tools that must be separated otherwise to avoid dings. The drawer could have a tray (D) for items that can be safely mixed.

be stored in this way. The more frequently used ones can stand in a rack on the wall, made from a block of wood with a series of holes drilled part way through.

The average drawer usually has its contents some way below the top. This indicates a use for a tray. The drawer itself may have a few large compartments, each for assorted tools that are not affected by being put together (Fig. 29-12C). The tray may be full size and be lifted out for access to the lower compartments, or it may be narrower so it can slide. A comparatively shallow tray (Fig. 29-12D) may take things like calipers, dividers, and templates. There could be fitted compartments for valuable precision tools, but generally it is sufficient to have a few main divisions. The bottom of the tray may have a covering of cloth or plastic.

Finishing

Items of the types described in this book will have to be finished in ways that are the same as, or compatible with, existing finishes of the room itself and things in it. It will not always be easy to identify existing finishes. Where investigation does not conclusively identify what has been used or even what the base wood is, it may be better to use a finish on the new work that is compatible the old than to try to get an exact match. A finish that does not quite achieve the match attempted is often less acceptable than one which is different than, but complementary to, the existing colors.

In general, it is usually unwise to mix more than two colors, except for white and black, which may be used sparingly in addition to other colors. A natural wood look, either genuine or simulated in plastic, may come alongside painted work, either directly or with a narrow line of black between. A bold color may be associated with a neutral or pastel shade of another color. People's tastes differ, and what may be too violent a contrast in the eyes of one viewer may be very attractive to another. Almost all combinations of color have been used by someone who regards the result as satisfactory, despite breaking all usual rules. If possible, try panels of the intended finishes in position and judge the effect before actually treating a piece of furniture.

For most furniture the beauty of the wood grain is the best decoration. It may be strained or given a clear finish. There are places where a painted finish is preferable, and then the basic material can be a cheaper and less attractive wood or a plain manufactured board.

There are not many items that can be left untreated. Because it is porous, wood absorbs dirt and becomes unattractive. There are just a few woods that contain natural oils and resins that give them a resistance to this. Teak for example, has an oil, and furniture made from it may be left untreated at first; but, later, treatment with special oil or polish will be needed. Some cedars contain a resin that makes them durable without treatment, but the appearance is not good enough for indoor furniture, and this wood is better used outdoors or in a shop.

WHY FINISH?

There are several reasons for applying a finish. The first is appearance. Attractive wood becomes more attractive under a clear glaze. It may look even better if a stain is used to bring out the beauty of the grain or emphasize the color.

Another reason for finishing is to give a surface that will facilitate cleaning. Without the protective finish, the wood might be marked by liquids and dirt. Bare wood is almost impossible to keep clean, even with frequent scrubbing—and that would not be appropriate for most furniture.

The finish may also be applied to prevent moisture absorption. This may not always be important especially if the furniture is always in an environment of equable temperature and humidity. Elsewhere, moisture absorption can cause expansion and contraction and warping. Most finishes seal the pores of the wood and reduce the absorption of moisture to a negligible amount.

Finishing may be done to give a uniform appearance. Even when a piece of furniture is made completely from the same wood, there can be variations in appearance. If different woods have to be used, something has to be done to give them a matching appearance, unless different colors are desired. There are stains and other treatments that make almost any final shade possible. A cheap wood can be made the same color as a more expensive wood, although its grain may show the expert that it is not genuine. Most staining is done to emphasize the existing color. For instance, the natural redness of some mahoganies can be deepened. It is unusual to use a color that is foreign to the wood. It is advisable to use stains normally associated with a wood unless special effects are required.

Painted finishes completely obscure the appearance of the wood or other material underneath. Their purpose is otherwise the same as for clear finishes: protection, waterproofing, and easy cleaning.

SURFACE PREPARATION

Whatever the finish, its final effect is largely dependent on the quality of the surface underneath. The actual application of the finish may be of much less importance. Although paint covers differences in color and shade, flaws left in the surface may become very apparent, particularly with a high-gloss paint.

Planing followed by thorough sanding is the usual way of preparing a surface. If the grain is the type that tears up no matter how it is planed, scraping should follow planing. If torn grain is dealt with by sanding only, not only is the process tedious, but the surface may be hollowed and the fibers bent instead of cut as they would be with a scraper. The eventual finish should be kept in mind during construction. Many parts are easily sanded before assembly, yet adequate sanding might be difficult later. Final sanding of exposed surfaces is best left until after assembly, when any risk of marking from construction work will have passed.

Although power sanding has its uses, final sanding is best done by hand, using abrasive paper wrapped around a block of wood or cork. The grade of abrasive should suit the wood and have sufficient cut to do what is intended. This means a coarse grade on softwoods, most of which soon clog fine papers. Sanding with the paper loose in the hand should only be done on curves. Final sanding of any surface should be in the direction of the grain. Looking across the wood toward a light will show any crosswise scratches that might show through a finish.

It may be necessary to use stoppings and fillers to get the wood to a satisfactory state. Although there are ways of making your own, it is probably wiser to buy them already prepared. Making your own really only pays when a large amount of furniture is being handled or there is no prepared material available.

Hollows where nails have been punched and similar small holes are best dealt with by a stopping, which is squeezed or pressed in the left to harden. Usually the top should stand very slightly above the surface so it can be leveled after it hardens. For larger cracks and places where joints may not fit as closely as you wish, there is Plastic Wood which is used similarly.

With some open-grained wood it is advisable to use a filler, otherwise the open grain and pores may show as minute holes and hollows in the finished surface. Most fillers are pastes. They are rubbed over the wood with a cloth and allowed to dry, then the surplus is sanded off.

Stoppings and fillers may take stain, or they may be obtained in colors to match the wood. For a painted finish there are stoppings which the makers advise using after the first coat of paint, not on bare wood. There are fillers for painted finishes which are used on very coarse-grained wood to hide the markings, but such woods are more likely to be used for exterior work than in built-in furniture.

STAINS

If the wood is to be stained, it is usual to use separate stains on the wood before applying the finish. There are colored varnishes and other finishes that might be considered to combine the processes, but the effect is not as good. A stain applied separately enhances the appearance of the wood as it penetrates the surface. With a colored varnish, the stain is in the finish and not the wood, so the grain is less enhanced. Also, as the varnish loses color with wear the appearance will be affected.

Stains may have water, spirits, or oil as solvents. A stain with an oil solvent is convenient. It soaks in to a good depth, and the color is even. It does not raise the grain. There is a slight risk of it seeping through some finishes.

Water stain comes as a powder to mix with water. Almost any shade or color is possible. As the water tends to raise the grain, it is advisable to dampen the surface with water as a preliminary treatment to get the grain raised in advance, then sand this after it has dried and before staining.

A spirit stain uses alcohol as the solvent, which makes it quick drying. This may be an advantage in some circumstances, but it makes staining a large area difficult, as parts will dry and causes streaks when new stain is brought alongside. A spirit stain is convenient for touching up and for treating carvings and moldings, but it is not a good choice for the overall staining of a large piece of furniture.

Prepared stains are usually provided with instructions, which should be followed, but it is always advisable to experiment on an inconspicuous part of the furniture or a scrap piece of the same wood. The color is affected by the original color of the wood and sometimes by chemicals in the wood. When a clear finish is applied, this may also alter the color slightly.

CLEAR FINISHES

Traditionally furniture was finished by waxes, oils, and resins. The beauty and patina of much old furniture is due more to use and polishing over the years than to the original surface treatment. Later, there was time when most furniture was French-polished (discussed later). In more recent years there have been brushed and sprayed finishes.

Waxing was once done with beeswax, and oiling was done with linseed oil. To get a satisfactory finish with these involves hard rubbing, then a pause of maybe a week and a repeat of the process, and so on for a long time. Neither process has much place in modern finishing of new work.

Shellac may be bought as flakes to dissolve in alcohol, or it can be bought already in solution. The natural color is orange-brown, but there is a bleached shellac more suitable for very light woods.

Shellac may be brushed on as a varnish. It will also act as a sealer under other finishes, closing the grain so the other solution does not soak in. It can also be used on resinous wood to prevent resin seeping through paint or some other finish. Even if shellac is not used all over a surface, brushing over knots is advisable before painting.

Shellac dries quickly. Quite a good brush finish can be obtained by applying up to six coats at about 2-hour intervals. The shellacked area can be rubbed with steel wool (or pumice stone) and oil to give an attractive, durable finish. Shellac applied by brush should be worked thinly and quickly to avoid problems of one part drying before an adjoining part if covered.

Shellac is also the material for *French polishing*. The polish (thinned shellac in alcohol) is put on a pad of batting (cotton or wool wadding), which is enclosed in a lint-free cloth. This is rubbed over the wood with a steady motion. At first the aim is to build up layers of polish. The rubbing motion causes the alcohol to evaporate quickly so the surface soon dries ready for another coat. When a sufficient surface has been built up, further steps are done with less polish and more friction bo build up a sheen on the surface. A spot of mineral oil may be added to the pad occasionally to prevent sticking. Later stages are done with the polish thinned still more.

VARNISH

In recent years there have been considerable changes in the makeup of varnishes and similar finishes. Some of the older varnishes, dependent on natural resins, would not dry properly, or their surface was affected if working conditions were not right. Modern synthetic varnishes are much less troublesome, but it is still advisable to work in a fairly warm, dry place and to avoid dust for at least a few hours. Some of these synthetic finishes may be described as furniture sealers as well as varnishes, but the results are similar.

Use a clean brush that has never been used for paint or other finishes. The slightest contamination with another finish may affect the appearance of varnish. It is usually helpful to warm the varnish before use, preferably by standing the can in hot water. Runs down the outside of the can can be avoided if a piece of wire is put across the can to wipe the brush against (Fig. 30-1A). Between coats, it is best to keep the brush suspended in varnish or thinners (Fig. 30-1B).

Read the directions on the can. Extensive brushing is inadvisable for synthetic varnishes, since it may cause air bubbles, which dry as little pinpoints in the surface. Some makers advise "flowing on" the varnish. This may be ideal from their point of view, but on anything except a horizontal surface, this will result in runs or curtains.

A first varnish coat may be thinned slightly to aid penetration of the wood. Thin sparingly—a very small amount of thinner has a surprising effect. The first coat may be brushed in several directions before finishing along the grain (Fig. 30-1C). Further coats should be brushed with just enough strokes to spread the varnish, almost entirely in the direction of the grain. In all cases, make a final brush stroke back towards the previsouly wetted area and lift the brush in one sweep as it passes over the area (Fig. 30-1D). This minimizes the risk of brush marks in the dried surface. On vertical or

Fig. 30-1. Preservation of brushes and the proper method of brushing are important in achieving the best paint or varnish finish.

sloping surfaces, work from the top, but let final brush strokes each time be upwards over the previously covered part.

Coats of varnish should be allowed to dry completely before applying more coats. In many cases, the surface may have to be left overnight before the next coat is applied. However, follow the maker's instructions. Formulas change, and there are some varnishes with which a following coat may come before complete hardening. Normally, when a coat has hardened, it should be rubbed down with steel wool or pumice. This removes any flaws and removes some of the gloss to give the next coat a better grip with less risk of runs. Any particles of abrasive or the dust they cause should be removed with a tack rag or a cloth moistened with thinner.

The number of coats needed will depend on the varnish and the desired finish. Usually the first coat soaks in, the next coat builds up somethings of a body, and the third coat shows what the finish is capable of. For some purposes, three coats may be enough, but the quality improves with a few further coats, providing rubbing down between coats is adequate.

LACQUER

Much commerically produced furniture has a sprayed-lacquer finish. Lacquer gives a hard, clear gloss that resists most of the usual conditions in the home. Lacquer is formulated with various ingredients, all of which dry quickly. There are brushing lacquers, but lacquers are most satisfactory when sprayed on.

Several coats can be sprayed on in a matter of hours. Lacquer should not be used with other finishes, since lacquer over most other finishes acts as a solvent and will soften or dissolve them to give an unsatisfactory result. Of course, skill is needed to get a satisfactory sprayed finish. Ripples on the surface may give an orange peel effect due to the spray not atomizing properly. Sags and runs are caused by an excess of lacquer. Blushing is caused by moisture in the lacquer.

PAINT

Like varnish, paint has undergone many changes in recent years. Of course, paint is basically varnish with colored pigment and a few other changes to suit the opaque finish, so changes brought by the introduction of synthestics affect paint as well as varnish. Use a complete paint system from one manufacturer so the different coats are compatible, and follow the directions of your chosen make.

The first coat of paint does little except to form a seal and to bond to the wood surface. Some hardboard and plywood makers recommend a sealer to use before the first coat of paint. This prevents excessive paint absorption. When nothing else is advised, the first coat should be a *primer* paint, much of which will soak in. This gives a good bond to the wood and reduces the risk of paint peeling at a future date.

There may have to be two priming coats on some very absorbent woods. The next coat is the *undercoat*. This has more body than the primer, and it dries with a matte surface ready for the *topcoat*. Many makers supply an undercoat paint of a color that matches the topcoat, but is not quite the same color. Thus there is little risk of missing a part, as there might be if both coats were exactly the same color.

Some surfaces may need two undercoats, rubbed down between coats. This is better than applying two topcoats. The topcoat, particularly if you use a gloss paint of the modern synthetic type, needs all the precautions mentioned for varnish. Spread enough to avoid runs and sags; finish strokes over previously wetted parts (going in the direction of the grain is not always essential). Usually it is better to make final strokes lengthwise on a panel. On a vertical or sloping surface, even when the length of a panel is the other way, it may be better to work from the top down and make final strokes upward, to reduce the risk of sags or runs.

Where there are molded edges, inset panels, carvings, or other shaped parts that adjoin flat panels, it is usually best to brush surplus paint or varnish onto the flat parts so as to remove paint away from the intricacies, which might trap excesses. If panels are painted first, there is nowhere for any excesses on the shaped parts to be spread.

If more than one color is to be used, the lighter one should be applied first. If it spreads to the area that is to be painted darker, it is more easily covered than a dark color under a light color. The best way to get neat joins between adjoining colors is to use masking tape, but make sure the paint the tape is stuck to is absolutely dry, or the tape may mar the surface.

If parts are to be given a clear finish, do this before painting nearby parts. Paint accidentally applied to bare wood will almost certainly leave a mark that will show through a clear finish, but if it splashed onto a clear-finished surface, it will wipe off without leaving a mark (providing it is not allowed to dry).

OTHER FINISHES

Veneer panels may be obtained to be ironed on or otherwise fixed to a surface. Formica and similar materials make good working surfaces, and these may be used directly on bare wood or used to supplement similar surfaces already on manufactured board.

There are decals that simulate inlays or other wood patterns. These are not popular with craftsmen any more than any imitation. However, nursery tale or other suitable decals may be used in a child's room. Usually it is advisable to apply all but the last coat of varnish and then fix the decal and give it time to dry before the final varnishing.

Self-adhesive flexible plastics are useful as shelf or interior linings and in places where stripping and replacing at some later date may be done, possibly for hygienic reasons. A suitably patterned piece may form a door panel, as could wall covering that matches that on the walls of the room.

There are plastic and cloth panels that could be used on furniture around a headboard or bar. Decorative plywood panels intended for walls may be included in furniture.

There are ways to make variations on the commoner finishes. Flock can be sprayed to give a clothlike finish. Lacquer can be treated to give crackle or wrinkle surfaces. Some of these treatments may harbor dirt and resist cleaning, so this should be considered before finishing wood in an unusual way.

Index